letters to my daughter

Nihara Guruge

letters to my daughter

a modern woman's quest

for purpose, identity and faith

nihara guruge

Letters To My Daughter by Nihara Guruge
Copyright © 2022 by Nihara Guruge
All Rights Reserved.
ISBN: 978-1-59755-711-5
All rights reserved

Published by: ADVANTAGE BOOKS™
                 Longwood, Florida, USA
                 www.advbookstore.com

Library of Congress Catalog Number: 2022943286

Name:	Guruge, Nihara, Author
Title:	*Letters To My Daughter*
	Nihara Guruge
	Advantage Books, 2022
Identifiers:	ISBN Paperback: 978159757115, Hardcover: 9781597557214 ebook: 9781597557313
Subjects:	Christian Life: Inspirational

First Printing: December 2022
20 21 22 23 24 25   10 9 8 7 6 5 4 3 2

dedication

To my daughters Liel and Adara, and every other daughter who reads this book;

"For this reason, since the day we heard about you, we have not stopped praying for you. We continually ask God to fill you with the knowledge of his will through all the wisdom and understanding that the Spirit gives, so that you may live a life worthy of the Lord and please Him in every way: bearing fruit in every good work, growing in the knowledge of God, being strengthened with all power according to his glorious might so that you may have great endurance and patience, and giving joyful thanks to the Father, who has qualified you to share in the inheritance of his holy people in the kingdom of light. For He has rescued us from the dominion of darkness and brought us into the kingdom of the Son He loves" - Colossians 1: 9-13

Nihara Guruge

table of contents

dedication 5

prologue 9

daughter

1. daughter, princess, royalty 17

2. father's hand, mother's breast 27

wife

3. nuptiae 41

4. refined 51

5. justified 63

mother

6. a mother is forged 73

7. a mother is born 85

worker

8. tapestry 99

9. faith in action 111

leader

10. breaking all the rules 123

11. a woman at work 135

12. a life of purpose.. 145

Nihara Guruge

prologue

One by one, they trooped into the board room, each selecting a comfortable chair until all but one seat was occupied. They looked around expectantly.

"Where is the lead guardian angel?" one attendee asked, almost impatiently, looking at her watch. There was a murmur in the room. No one knew.

Suddenly the door burst open, and an extremely tired-looking angel rushed in with a stack of papers and gratefully slid into the empty chair.

"Right," the angel that looked to be the chairperson said, "Better late than never. Let's begin. If everyone has read the pre-read, you would know why we are gathered here today. We need to decide on the best course of action to…" he trailed off looking at one angel who had gotten up from the table.

"So sorry, just grabbing a cup of coffee, don't mind me," the disrupter said as he tried to magically feign invisibility in his pursuit of refreshments and failing miserably.

"Right…RIGHT, so as I was saying, we need to decide on the best course of action to get Nihara to write this book, or to put it more accurately, finish writing it."

The chairperson headed to the whiteboard that mysteriously appeared. "Let's workshop this. No need to invent the wheel here. What has worked in the past?"

One angel piped in proudly, "well, remember the time she wasn't sure she wanted children, or to be specific, she was dead set against it? I had the idea to send that pastor to speak to her directly at the altar! Now I hear she's even pregnant with her second child". He sat back, looking quite proud.

The lead guardian angel hurriedly scanned through his papers. With a tired voice, he countered, "Well, that didn't exactly work immediately - it still took about two more years of bombarding her with the Abrahamic covenant and other messages from pastors across continents before she even started to think that maybe she should have children. We don't have that kind of time here".

The chairperson started scribbling something on the whiteboard but proceeded to strike it off.

"What about moving to a new country? She had doubts about that but eventually said yes?"

The lead angel referred to his notes again. "Looks like we sent a visitor from that country to their local church in Texas on the same weekend they said they would pray and ask for guidance. It was random and bizarre enough to get her attention. It seemed like...a sign," he said with some distaste, clearly no great fan of the human obsession with signs.

"Okay, great," the chairperson replied, scribbling furiously on the whiteboard. "So clearly, the direct approach worked best. Where is she now? Who is preaching this Sunday? Let's send him a message or vision or whatever when the time comes. He can speak to her directly".

The secretary started to write down the action item on his notepad.

"And better not make it too cryptic. As plain as possible. Tell her...tell her that she is sitting at a writing table writing this book."

One angel wrinkled her nose in distaste. "Isn't that a bit...tacky? It seems to lack creativity or dramatic symbolism."

The meeting was over, and the lead guardian angel had already started to get up from his chair when he replied curtly, "Unless we want to be back here in another week to rework this, let's keep this as simple as possible. No cryptic messages" and departed swiftly.

Taking that to mean the end of the meeting, the remaining angels trooped out hurriedly before the chairperson could add anything to the agenda.

The account above is, needless to say, entirely fictional, but it amuses me sometimes to imagine that these things take place to give us the occasional nudge we need in the right direction. I first felt the idea for this book land in my heart in 2019, with only the title of the book, "Letters to my Daughter," clear in my thoughts. I was not even pregnant at the time and thought that it was a book written for the metaphorical daughter, in the sense that we are all daughters. Within two months, I was pregnant, and I discovered I was having a girl a few months later. The two years that followed were an intense season of my life that seemed to take me apart and rebuild the very core of me. A constant thought I had throughout, whether it was about postpartum struggles or marriage, was, 'I wish I knew this going in.' So, I decided to bare my soul to my daughter, knowing that the opportunity to do so was a gift. After all, our days on earth are numbered, and there is no guarantee of tomorrow.

I confess, after a few chapters, I got distracted by life and started to think that this was a pet project that was optional and hence could be shelved. Perhaps more significant was that I did not know how to write this book without being drastically more vulnerable than I was comfortable with, to levels I felt were embarrassing. I was busy with my career and my family and welcomed an excuse to hide away my secret project. I told myself, 'this was just something I wanted to do; it wasn't something I had to do.' I lacked the courage to finish. This was when my fictional account with the angels took place, as God had to give me a less-than-subtle nudge.

I was attending Sunday service while visiting my parents in Sri Lanka, and my active toddler kept me extremely busy at the back of the hall. It was the end of service, and the minister had started to pray for individuals. Suddenly I heard him speak directly to me. He spoke of seeing me sitting at a writing desk, writing a book, and went on to describe the vision. I was shaken to the core. As soon as we were in the car on our way home, I confronted my mom, almost accusatory, asking, "did you tell him I was writing a book?!". She replied coolly, "No, Nihara, I don't go around talking about your hobbies," implying that she had much more riveting topics to converse around than me.

Nonetheless, it was the nudge I needed, but more importantly, the courage I needed to allow myself to be this vulnerable in the chapters to follow, if for nothing else other than obedience. I am a fallible human being and a first-time author, so I ask that you think of me kindly as you read on. Like you, I'm just trying to figure it out, one step at a time, and doing my best to stay the course. Scripture says that "your word is a lamp unto my feet," and that is what writing this book has felt like; I had no book outline or even plan for what I would and would not say, but I had to rely on God to feed my thoughts chapter by chapter and see what shaped up. The result is what you have in your hands right now.

As you know only too well, women play many significant roles throughout our lives, some of them being mother, wife, and daughter, and for those employed or engaging in some form of business, as employees and leaders in our own right in the marketplace. The book is divided into five main sections that represent some of the seasons in my life or even roles that I have had to assume in my life. While we do so much more, these were the roles I felt were most used by God to draw me closer to Him and grow and challenge my innermost character.

I believe these seasons in my life are worth sharing with my daughters, and I have allowed myself the privilege of looking into every aspect of my life accordingly. My goal is not to fit into a self-help category in a bookstore. Instead, to share some intimate parts of my journey in the hope that at least some nugget would help you in your own path, which may or may not look like mine. After all, while we women are on our own unique paths in life, we are also somewhat on the same journey, bound together by our womanhood, motherhood, or sisterhood.

The late Dr. Billy Graham said, "The Bible is God's love letter to us." I confess that this was not how I approached the Bible for most of my life. I had tried everything to read the Bible more consistently; I threw money at it by buying 'better' Bibles and devotionals, hoping it would tell me which part of the Bible to read and when. I even excused my behavior with the 'story' approach. I convinced myself that given my Christian upbringing, I knew most of the bible stories anyway, so unlike a new believer, what new stories are there for me to learn? In the end, it took the conviction of the spirit to make me wake up one day and say, given that I was an avid reader, the least I could do it is to treat it as a book to be read from cover to cover. So, I downloaded the Bible app and signed onto a 365-bible reading plan. Living in Singapore at that time, I had my morning and evening commute in the comfortable subways to get through a day's worth of reading – usually requiring no more than 15 minutes. So

I started, and could meet the fifteen-minute obligation on most days. It started as a chore to get out of the way before I could listen to my music which filled my commute.

Unsurprisingly, half the time, I was distracted as there is nothing quite as distracting as a bus ride or a train ride when you are trying to focus. Sometimes I even had to re-read a chapter because I realized I had come to the end of the page without recollecting what I had just read. But I persisted, and then slowly, something began to change. Instead of a one-sided read, it started to become a conversation. I started to hear thoughts, ideas, and even revelations of what verses could mean in my life and in an absolute sense for the world. I started to get insights into situations I was to face ahead of me that day or even for that week. The more I read, the more I wanted to read. It felt like a tall cool glass of water on a hot summer day. It has guided me through impossible situations both at work and in my personal life, speaking even when I was not actively conscious of it.

Do you ever hear a song on the radio or on your playlist that immediately makes you think of a particular moment in time, maybe dancing with your friends, perhaps a music festival, or even an ex-boyfriend? These promises and passages have been like that to me over the last decade of my life, representing highs, lows, and everything in between. I have attempted to tie those passages to my stories to give a voice not just to my musings but as a reminder that God is not just the Yahweh of the Old Testament but is very much alive today and speaks actively to those willing to converse and listen.

Nihara Guruge

daughter

Nihara Guruge

1. daughter, princess, royalty

"I have loved you with an everlasting love; I have drawn you with unfailing kindness" -Jeremiah 31:3

What would your answer be if I asked you to name a great love story? My husband, who is a hopeless romantic, would probably pick 'The Notebook,' a movie that may even extract a few tears from him at every showing. Personally, I love superhero movies and would have hoped that if my life was made into a movie, it would be of the action-packed super-heroine genre where I regularly fly in to save the day. But under extreme duress, I would admit that my second favorite genre would be epic love stories, preferably movies set in a historical period before the invention of penicillin.

The truth is, we have been created for love, to love, and to be loved. Our souls crave it, something even Hollywood producers have caught onto. Just this year alone, hundreds of movies with romantic storylines will be released around the world, and a single person's life span will not be enough to watch every romance movie ever made. How often I have wished to be the heroine, on an adventure, finding love and romance! And yet, these movies are just shadows of the first, original, deepest romantic tale spanning all of time, where the pursuer says to you (and me), 'I have loved you with an everlasting love.' As a woman, we can perhaps imagine ourselves being pursued, desired, cherished, and wanted, even more than men. I have been blessed in life, having known parents, grandparents, sister, husband, and other friends and family whose love I have experienced. And yet, as strong and wonderful as that love is, no one has loved me with an everlasting love in the way God has loved me. No one has loved me since the beginning of time or pursued me through the ages with the ultimate sacrifice, His Son, to reunite me into his presence. No one, knowing ahead of time every single mistake, sin, and failure I would make in life, would die for me, so I could be saved and set free to join Him, just to have a relationship with me.

My story, which I will pour out to you in the following letters, is a love story where God has pursued me and continues to pursue me daily, just as He is pursuing you. Women play many roles in this world, but let us never forget that first and foremost, we are daughters of God, loved, cherished, and pursued through the times.

Pursued

"For He chose us in Him before the creation of the world to be holy and blameless in his sight. In love He predestined us for adoption to sonship through Jesus Christ, in accordance with his pleasure and will" -Ephesians 1: 4-5

"Everyone, please take a pen and piece of paper and draw out the most significant moments in your life, moments that affected you deeply and resulted in who you are today. Remember pictures, not words! When you are finished, we will share your results with the group". It was a beautiful sunny day as far as I could tell through the windows in the conference room, though one could hardly tell given that we were all bundled up due to the air-conditioning, no doubt blasting at a level that is not needed or recommended. Upon glancing about, a few colleagues seemed to be suppressing eye-rolls while the more earnest participants were already scribbling furiously on their paper pads. I tried to focus on the task at hand, staring at the blank piece of paper and chewing on my pen absently. The ask was clear and not unusual for a corporate team-building event. The answer, my most honest answer, was obvious to me. That Sunday was scorched into my memory, never to be forgotten. But it didn't feel like the right setting to share something so intimate or so personal. It didn't feel professional. I pushed back the memory of that day to the back of my mind and scribbled some pictures depicting my family, Sri Lanka, Singapore, a Squash Racquet, and sat back. That should be good enough for the facilitator.

To anyone who asks, I would always respond that I was born into an ordinary middle-class family in Sri Lanka, a small but beautiful, developing island just south of India. I was a daughter to two wonderful parents (still married after three and a half decades) who did everything within their power to ensure my sister and I had all we needed, including our best possible chance at a better future. Like my mother and her mother before her, I attended a Catholic convent school, was taught about God, took my first Holy Communion before I hit ten years of age, and memorized the books of the Bible for Religious Studies. My mother religiously took my sister and me to church every Sunday, though I can't remember being anything but an unwilling participant. If I were being honest, growing up, I would only think of God when I needed something, whether it was exams or protection, so I suppose to the kid that I was, God was more of a genie to grant wishes than anything else.

As High school came around and thoughts of university entered our consciousness, it felt natural to pack my schedule with two types of Advanced Level exams, school activities, and sports. Logically, or so I thought, Sunday church attendance would need to be dropped to make room for Math and Chemistry classes, and evenings were cleared in favor of school activities and squash training. I had always felt different, and though I had some wonderful friendships that are strong to this day, surviving time zones and continents, I felt alone, a feeling only exacerbated by an intense schedule that put me on a different path from the rest of my family and my friends. Though I probably sound no more unique than the average teenager, I had an enormous chip on my shoulders that embittered me towards my family and the world and fueled a furious desire to conquer it. The child-like wonder I had of God when I was a small girl was but a distant memory of the past. Perhaps, like everyone else, I was just craving love, attention, and appreciation but anticipating that I would not receive what I so desperately wanted, I hardened my heart, focusing intensely on activities and accomplishments.

Against this backdrop, I could honestly say that when I left Sri Lanka at eighteen to attend university in another country, I did so with no intention of ever looking or coming back. Perhaps here, I would find what I was looking for, though even I did not know what that was. I boarded at one of the Halls closest to my classes, where it wasn't unusual to find a smaller group of foreign students milling around the Hall cafeteria during the weekends when the locals usually went home to see their families. On one particular weekend during that first semester, I was sitting down for dinner with two other foreign students staying in the same hall. I'm unsure how the conversation turned in the direction it did, but before I knew it, I had an invitation to go to church with them on Sunday. It was an easy yes from me. Despite my chosen lifestyle, I did believe in God, even though it has been a long time since we had a heart-to-heart.

When I woke up that Sunday, I had no reason to guess it would be anything other than another Sunday, that instead, it would be one for the books. That years later, as I sat in a cold conference room trying to think of one of the most defining moments in my life, it would be that Sunday that I would think about. Oblivious to all that awaited me, I walked into that church and sat down with my friends, off-center from the stage. This was by far the largest church I had been to all my life (looking back now, having seen entire stadiums filled with believers, I chuckle at how large that hall seemed to me at the time!). The band came on, and everyone started to sing.

Somewhere between the first and second songs, something happened that, to this day, I can't explain very well. I just sat down in my seat, which in itself was unusual, considering that the entire hall of over a thousand people were on their feet, clapping and singing. For the first time in years, I started to cry.

I'm not sure who was more surprised, my friends or I, at crying, for no apparent reason, in the middle of a crowd of what I can imagine was a thousand people (I had always been the cool, confident, sarcastic type-hardly the type to break down and cry). But after all those years of knowing *of* God, *of* Jesus, it was as if, for the first time in my life, He was suddenly right there in front of me, so real, telling me that He loved me and He has waited for me, and that I was His and that I was not alone. Everything else around me melted away, and a dam inside me broke, the sweeping water washing away and breaking down every barrier and wall which was carefully constructed and held up by hurt and rejection.

If I had to explain it, the best I can do is to say that up to this point in my life, I had been underwater, my hearing muffled, my breathing restricted, my vision clouded by the fogginess of the water, and suddenly, at that moment, I broke through the surface, to take in a full gasp of air, to feel the sun on my skin, and to see the sun and the sky clearly for the first time in my life.

What would follow that fateful day can only be described as the journey of a lifetime. I didn't become a different person overnight, but with almost eighteen years of hindsight since that day, I can more clearly see that God has gently guided me through situations, strongholds, challenges, highs, and lows, but always in one direction; towards Him. Over time He has restored all of my relationships, instructed me, shown me truths about His provision, and is more real to me today than ever. Every time I stumble and fall, I remember there isn't a mistake I can make on earth that can separate me from Him. I was loved unconditionally. The following letters will only be a glimpse of what He has done and continues to do in my life.

Daughter, I also feel compelled to share this story because I believe that the reason that God allowed me to attend that university, against all odds, as I would describe later, was so that I could sit at that table during dinner that weekend, and receive an invitation to go back to church. I believe God was pursuing me then, and He is still pursuing me, years and decades later, and that is what makes my life the greatest love story I would ever personally encounter in this lifetime.

Lost and Found Again

"For this son of mine was dead and is alive again; he was lost and is found. So, they began to celebrate" -Luke 15:24

There is a well-known story in the Bible about a wealthy man with two sons. Though well-loved and provided for, one son asks the father for his inheritance and, after taking it, leaves home to squander it recklessly. Soon, he is left with nothing and is so destitute that he is forced to work as a hired hand for a pig farmer. He is so hungry and desperate that he is tempted to eat the food given to the pigs. With regret, he realizes that even the servants in his father's house had better living conditions. He has given up his inheritance and does not feel worthy of being his father's son anymore, so he resolves to go home and beg his father to be a servant in his household instead. The gospel of Luke goes on to say:

"So he got up and went to his father. But while he was still a long way off, his father saw him and was filled with compassion for him; he ran to

his son, threw his arms around him, and kissed him. The son said to him, 'Father, I have sinned against heaven and against you. I am no longer worthy to be called your son. But the father said to his servants, 'Quick! Bring the best robe and put it on him. Put a ring on his finger and sandals on his feet. Bring the fattened calf and kill it. Let's have a feast and celebrate. For this son of mine was dead and is alive again; he was lost and is found.' So, they began to celebrate." -Luke 15: 20-24

If I had to name one regret in life, if it were indeed possible to have regrets, I would name two from my youthful days. The first was when I started working full-time as a graduate and suddenly, going to church on Sunday became too much of a commitment to bear. I longed instead to spend my weekend with my friends, basking in my newfound financial freedom. Slowly, the weekday gathering was dropped due to long work hours, and eventually, once a week on Sunday turned into twice a month and then none at all. I had seen God baffle the mind with His generosity in my life, but I was quick to forget. With my waning faithfulness, I made my second mistake; deciding to take my love life into my own hands. I can't speak for everyone; I feel the pursuit of love is one area where it is tough to be patient and wait on the Lord. Perhaps that is because, unlike jobs, there always seem to be open doors beckoning you to walk through; or perhaps it is because of our innate desire for love and connection. Or maybe it is because we rarely think that we will find a partner who can fulfill all our physical, relational, and spiritual needs; therefore, when we find someone who meets one or two of the three, we settle. Ultimately it is because we credit ourselves for doing a better job of playing matchmaker than we do God. Whatever the reason, even though who you decide to marry, who you choose to be your companion for the rest of your life, for better or for worse, is the single biggest decision you would ever make in your life, with the ability to affect your emotions, body, finances, spirituality and even lifestyle, it is also the one which tends to be the least thought through; at least, that was the case for me.

This was the only relationship I had before the one with my husband. He was a wonderful man, a 'catch' even. But he did not share my faith and belief in Jesus, which had fundamentally transformed my very existence during university. Inevitably I allowed myself to make choices that, even in the moment, I regretted immediately. Perhaps the most illuminating hint should have been that the closer I got to him, the further I felt from God, not because God had moved away from me, but because I was hiding my face in shame, unable to even pray to God, thinking that I am not worthy to be heard.

One afternoon, my mother was driving me somewhere in Sri Lanka, and out of the blue, she told me, *"Nihara, just because we have met his parents, you don't have to feel pressured to get married",* a statement perhaps only South Asians would understand fully. I received that comforting message unemotionally, but I believe it was the last piece of courage I needed to let the relationship run its course. I thank God for mothers and their perceptions. I have only started to appreciate how in-tune moms are to the emotional state of their babies after having a daughter of my own. Moms can pick up on the slightest change in our children's mood, temperament, and emotions, and I think my mother was able to sense that something was not right with me.

"And you also were included in Christ when you heard the message of truth, the gospel of your salvation. When you believed, you were marked in him with a seal, the promised Holy Spirit." - Ephesians 1:13

I was not faithful to God, but we are promised that once we accept Jesus into our hearts and lives, we are 'sealed' by the Holy Spirit, where God marks us as His own, stamping on us a seal of protection, ownership, and sonship. Even when I had turned away, even when I was running away, just like the prodigal son in the story, I was still His daughter with a crown on my head. I just had to remind myself of that fact. As much as I had done my best to rule myself out of my position in life as a daughter of God, a princess, and a co-heir in His Kingdom, nothing can separate me from him now because I accepted that Jesus was my God and savior. And so, it was only a matter of time before what was a quiet prick to my conscience about the choices I had made, the disquiet in my soul soon became a deafening roar, inciting a conviction in me of what I needed to do. It wasn't too late; I needed to go back to God. And He welcomed me with open arms.

"Trust in the LORD with all your heart and lean not on your own understanding; in all your ways submit to Him, and He will make your paths straight." - Proverbs 3:5-6

While I was going through this crisis of faith, halfway across the world (literally), and unbeknownst to me, the man who would one day become my husband was bewildered at his own share of closed doors. Born and raised in Houston, Texas, he was one of the tens of thousands of employees of the same company I worked for. The probability of our paths ever crossing was slim to none. Later, he would reminisce with me about how, at the time, the door or two that closed for him around this time did not make sense. They should have been easy opportunities for him to secure; one was in Canada, another in Kuwait. The door that did open for him, unexpectedly, I might add, was to Singapore, a place he had not even been thinking of. Ten thousand miles later, through mutual friends, we became acquainted and became friends.

When we started dating, I braced myself to have a difficult discussion with him about 'doing things the right way.' Still, despite my trepidation given our widely different social values and cultures, he agreed easily. Being a Christian himself, we started attending church together, growing in our faith together. We would experience a growth spurt in our spiritual lives in the coming years, finding community and even going on a mission trip together in Asia, which was a life-changing experience for both of us. Ten years later, he is not just my life companion and partner but my best friend. Years into our marriage, when the storms came and the wind beat down on our home, it would be the conviction that we both had that God has brought us together and is a part of our marriage even as we both seek him individually and together, that would allow our home to take a few strong hits, but remain standing (albeit needing a fresh coat of paint and a wall or two if I was being honest).

It is easy, maybe even comforting, to think that our choices don't have an impact beyond our immediate life, but daughter, even your smallest of decisions can have a generational impact. My grandmother is a truly extraordinary woman who I always thought had the misfortune to be born into the wrong decade. If she had been born in the twenty-first century in a different country, she may have been a CEO or a businesswoman of some form, as she is truly a formidable force. As it is, what she was allowed to do, all she was raised to do, was to be a wife and mother, something she did with extraordinary grace and love. I once asked her how she met our grandfather and how they dated and decided to get married. She shocked me by saying that she almost did not marry him until he agreed that their children would be raised as Christians, which was important to her at the time. That one choice of hers resulted in two generations of Christian men and women (three if I count our children) who have been following Jesus.

So my darling daughter, when it comes to who you might decide to walk through life with, or whether you choose a partner at all, choose wisely, choose prayerfully, and most of all, always choose God, who will never let you down. As the letters to follow will illuminate, it could be one of the most important decisions you ever make in your life, potentially leaving its mark for generations to come. But above all, take heart! Your good father knows you better than you know yourself, and just as my mother desired nothing more than what was best for me, He is looking out for you and has a great purpose laid out for you. Just stay close to him and brace yourself for an adventure of a lifetime.

2. father's hand, mother's breast

"I know your deeds. See, I have placed before you an open door that no one can shut. I know that you have little strength, yet you have kept my word and have not denied my name" -Revelations 3:8

As I walked along the temporary booths set up at the career fair with my mother, barely seventeen years old, I could not help but be overwhelmed. I would be exaggerating if I said that I had the foresight to bring myself to that fair or even had a clue about what would happen once I graduated from High School. The reality was that around the time I was 15 or 16, while I was busy with enough academics, sports, and extra-curricular activities to fill my day, I was hardly thinking of what might lay beyond. We didn't have school counselors or career days at our schools growing up, as students typically get assigned university tracks based on their high school A-Level results. My mother, however, had been researching options for my further education and had come across this fair, whereby foreign universities would prop up tents to attract Sri Lankan students in the hope that they eventually become skilled immigrants. This was unsurprising, as the country, through an advanced education system, often produced more students proficient in math and sciences than its free but limited number of local university spots could hold.

We were, on average, a middle-class family in a developing country, perhaps even considered poor by comparison with the wealth in the USA. My parents had sunk most, if not all, of their savings into our house, my sister, and me. At times we struggled financially though our parents did their best to shield us, so much so that it was only as a working adult that I fully appreciated how much stress my parents must have been under in our formative years. And so, it was quite audacious of my mother and perhaps a testament to her faith to dream so big as to think that I could afford to attend a university in another country. I often attribute the blessings and miracles of my earlier years to her faith rather than my own. It certainly wasn't any answer to my prayers as I had long since stopped attending church, not to mention abandoned prayer. I far preferred to rely on my capabilities and strengths to get desired outcomes.

Daughter, I hope what I share after this will encourage you if and when you become a mother one day. There is a force to be reckoned with when a mother cares for, prays for, and believes in and on behalf of her children. I certainly found that to be the case. All my mother knew and desired was a better life and better opportunities for her two daughters, though we had no clear pathway at that point as to how we could finance either my tuition or living expenses or flights on my parent's income. It was one thing to take care of a family in Sri Lanka, with its access to great education and healthcare practically free of charge, but it was a whole other dream to think of attending a university in a foreign country. But she believed. And on a sunny day (we rarely had any other kind of day in Sri Lanka), we found ourselves at that fair. We may have attended more than one booth, but there were only two that I recall. Possibly, my mother is very much like me, abhorrent to long stretches of shopping, and had decided in her impatience to hone into the booth of her choice, namely the top university in Singapore at the time, The National University of Singapore.

After a short conversation, the booth representative made a remarkable comment; "This university is really hard to get into, even with your grades and activities and sports– why don't you try another less competitive option, perhaps that university down there?" I can only hope the school has been sending down better ambassadors to the country since this incident. But the message was clear; perhaps he knew something we didn't. Maybe this dream was just too far-reaching. We gathered what information we could, visited the other booths, and headed home. Neither my mother nor I had any intention of being told what to do (and, in this case, being told what not to do), and months later, I applied to NUS against his well-meaning but unwelcome advice.

"But God chose the foolish things of the world to shame the wise and the weak things of the world to shame the strong. God chose the lowly things of this world and the despised things—and the things that are

not—to nullify the things that are, so that no one may boast before him." -1 Corinthians 1: 27-29

While the university ambassador I met on that fated day at the fair was entitled to his opinion, God had other ideas. Months later, God opened a door for me in the form of a large manila envelope, too big and too thick to be anything other than a congratulatory message. As I stared at the words, "Congratulations, we are pleased to inform you...." on the NUS letterhead, the rest of the words faded away as my mouth opened in disbelief. In hindsight, I should have let my mother open that envelope as it was even more of an answered prayer for her than it was for me. Years later, I realized that a mother's prayer has a special power and significance. While I had always prayed, nothing made me pray as much as I did from the moment that I became pregnant, knowing God heard each of those prayers whispered over my daughter in the middle of the night, in the early morning hours or when I am by myself, sometimes nothing more than a desperate "Please God, keep our baby safe."

I had been accepted, but it was still unclear to me exactly how I would be able to afford to attend the university of my choice. Somehow, through some miracle, and a combination of the maximum amount of financial aid available, gifts from loved ones, and perhaps even gifts from those who were merely acquaintances (that is the kind of communal spirit that makes me miss Sri Lanka so fondly when I remember it), I was able to pack up all my clothes, and even some bedding into one suitcase and made that first trip to the country which would become my home for the next fifteen years.

It was in this university that I would sit at the table, which had the exact hall mates, who asked me which church I attended, and upon hearing the negative, took me to the exact church where God met me again, at the ripe old age of eighteen.

Unfortunately, the financial aid was insufficient to fund a critical piece of equipment that was a staple of university life; a personal computer. Despite all God has done for me up to this point by way of provision, what transpires next is probably what I best remember when I start to doubt His ability to provide for even the smallest need or the creativity with which He can orchestrate events to meet those needs. My Aunt, who to this day is one of the most resourceful forces of nature I have ever met, looked far and wide within her extensive network of contacts (no doubt at my mother's urging) and was able to find a Sri Lankan residing in Singapore. I was looking for his support to guarantee a loan so I could purchase the laptop, but he ended up buying me a laptop computer as a gift. In 2005, I was the proud owner (and one of the relatively early adapters) of a Macintosh computer. Two years later, in 2007, Steve Jobs announced the release of the first iPhone. That laptop lasted almost eight years, only to be replaced when my then-boyfriend, now husband, nudged me and said, "it's time to let go." What need was too small or too insignificant for God to provide?

For the next four years, God continued to meet my financial needs through my parents, who provided me with a stipend allowance of about USD 200 per month to fund all my expenses; meals, transportation, incidentals, etc. Anything extra would need to be earned through part-time gigs such as ushering or tuition. As most students on a budget would tell you, this often means a Nutella sandwich as a substitute for meals, sometimes days at a time. Four years later, I was able to graduate from University, as did many of my peers at the time, though I did so with a hefty tuition loan balance hanging over my head.

However, the timing of my graduation was less than ideal because, by the spring of 2009, the world was reeling from the global financial crisis that had been breaking up the sector since 2008—a truly unfortunate time to be a Finance graduate. Jobs were scarce, and while many of my friends had to either embark on yet further education to wait out the recession or leave the country upon expiration of their student visas, Singapore's economy, undoubtedly through the government's prudent management following lessons learned during the previous Asian financial crisis, was still somewhat alive; or in amateur medical terms, there was at least, still a heartbeat, albeit a distressed. Unsurprisingly most companies froze or drastically reduced hiring. I kept hearing story after story of my peers in business school, even those at the top of the cohort, getting their job offers rescinded by banks and financial institutions.

Against the backdrop of such dim prospects, I felt I should at least try to apply to a handful of companies that I felt truly passionate about. Nothing special about me could single me out as an applicant when so many more talented students and recently laid-off graduates of earlier cohorts were also applying; I wasn't even at the top of my class. But I applied to a handful of companies anyway, with one being at the top of my list and close to my heart. If I could not get a job, I would be forced to leave the country and likely default on my debt, given the significantly lower salary levels in Sri Lanka.

Two Copper Coins

"Bring the whole tithe into the storehouse, that there may be food in my house. Test me in this," says the Lord Almighty, "and see if I will not throw open the floodgates of heaven and pour out so much blessing that there will not be room enough to store it" - Malachi 3:10

Giving to the less fortunate was always something that was ingrained in me from a young age, with one of my oldest memories being that my father always gave something to the beggars on the street, almost every day, even (I think) when he could not afford to do so. My mother's giving of the tithe, which is a commitment to give ten percent of one's income to God, was less visible, and so it was only after I became a Christian that I was introduced to the concept. As a new believer, I wanted to honor the practice, but it was a difficult choice, and I had plenty of reasons not to do it; my monthly allowance was already stretched. I ate what meals my hostel gave, but the allowance was meant to cover all other food, travel, and miscellaneous expenses. I had extra income from odd jobs I did around the university, but with the number of school activities I had to do to continue to qualify for hostel stay, Varsity Squash, Soccer, Track, and Drama Club, to name a few, I was running on fumes with days beginning early in the morning before dawn and ending late at night. Most days, my breakfast was a slice of egg toast and chocolate milk, lunch was fish and chips from the canteen, and dinner was provided in the hostel. Thank goodness for affordable food prices in University canteens! I illustrate this not to elicit pity, as a dismal number of people in the world have far less, but to convey that in this context, parting with USD20 a month was not easy. That was over fifteen breakfasts or almost ten lunches! I even argued that this was not my money or income, as it belonged to my mother. Or that I should wait until I have a good job before I start tithing.

All arguments failed, and my desire to tithe overcame all perceived challenges. I wholeheartedly believed that my monthly allowance was a blessing from God, and the least I could do to honor Him and thank Him for it was to show Him that I trusted him with a measly 10% of it. Further, this particular verse in Malachi is the only time in the Bible where God asks us to test Him; at the very least, I was intellectually intrigued. He sounded very confident in what he was promising he could do in exchange for the tithe from me. And so I started, with great difficulty at first but slowly, with consistency. I believe I tithed most months, if not all, during my university life, and at the time I was applying for jobs, it had become somewhat of a habit for almost four years.

Against this backdrop, I approached graduation surrounded by dismal reports of the market outlook, a contracting economy, and job losses most heavily hitting the field of my expertise. A few months after graduation, I received a call I was not expecting from a large multinational company (which was my top choice for employment) asking me to come in for the recruitment assessment. Would you believe I chose that particular month to skip a tithe after all this? What is even more hilarious is that by total coincidence or divine intervention, I got a call from the recruiter informing me that my assessment day had been postponed shortly after that. Whatever the reason, from that month in 2009 onwards, I have never missed a tithe to this day.

The assessment day arrived, an otherwise unremarkable day, and I went down to the center. We're not given details of what to expect, part of the assessment being the measure of capacity, which is to say, how we would digest any new information or tasks on the spot to achieve outcomes. I walked in and saw that the group consisted of myself and seven other gentlemen (if I may use the term loosely to describe recent graduates such as myself). I did not feel intimidated, but I did wonder about my odds and how on earth I was selected to be here. No one has accused me of undue humility in my life, but even I had to admit that despite my all-rounded CV, I was not a government scholar famed for their perfect grades. I was also the only woman of color in the room. Over the last four years, I had experienced enough prejudice and stereotypes often endured by ethnic minorities in the country, which meant I was far from confident that I would get a fair assessment. Still, I was competitive enough to give it my best and ended the day thinking I had a real shot at being in the top 2-3 applicants. This was followed by a few weeks of anticipation when one day, as I was with my friends, I received a call from an unknown number. The recruiter gave me detailed feedback on my performance (thank you, but can we skip to the end?) and ended the call with, 'we would like to offer you a graduate opportunity.'

The other graduates had been calling each other to find out who got the job, and one of them eventually called me. Once I told him I got the position, his first words were, "We figured if one of us didn't get it, you would be the one to get it as you were the only woman, and they probably wanted a woman for diversity." I didn't realize the significance and depth of the discrimination in the words at the time. Only time and maturity will enlighten me on that. If he was right (and I believe he wasn't), then I'm grateful it worked in my favor, with no hard feelings. My thoughts, however, were elsewhere, marveling, "God, how great are you?!"

There is an account in the Bible of Jesus hanging around with the disciples at the temple, and they happened to observe many people coming in to give their offerings to the temple treasury. He witnessed many rich people give large sums of money, probably without blinking an eye, given their wealth. Then a poor widow came along and put in two small copper coins, and Jesus said she put in more than the rich because what she gave cost her more. The two small copper coins she gave were all she had, probably far more than ten percent, as widows had no income at those times. My $20 tithe a month felt small, paltry, and insignificant to me in the context of some big numbers that the church was able to collect given their large, rich congregation, but it cost me a lot to give. More importantly, it was all God asked for as a show of faith, not because He needed it, but because He could use that $20 to "throw open the windows of heaven and rain down so many blessings that there is no room to contain them." This is the only passage in the Bible where God says, "you don't have to take me at my word. You can test me and see if I will not be true to my word."

And daughter, let me tell you, He is up to the challenge. He had thrown open the heavens so many times in my life; even when my husband and I have gone through periods where it felt like one thing after the other was draining our savings account, I have never had to check my bank balance to see if I had enough. He has provided for me so much that I have been able to increase my paltry $20 tithe many times over, so much so that my husband and I do not feel the need to be limited to a 10% tithe. I could pay off student loans in two to three years, get jobs during recessions, meet my partner in Christ in my husband, who shared and surpassed my tithing habits, and enjoy a smooth pregnancy and birth with my daughter, among countless other blessings. In fact, between my husband and I, between 2018-2022 due to various restructuring efforts, relocations, and recessions, we kept taking turns having to look for a job at least six times. But through these all, we have seen God come through for us miraculously and keep providing for our needs through opportunities and promotions. Giving my tithe is now one of my favorite parts of my month, which represents a moment of thanks for all He has blessed me with, and also a wink and a nod to God when I ask Him, "what's next?" Most of all, whenever life throws me a curve ball or something looks to come to erode our way of life, I can demand a conversation with God, boldly and confidently, just as a daughter will come to her Father and say, "God, you know I tithe, so you will have to show up for me here because otherwise, your word would not be true." So far, He is yet to let me down.

The Hair on our Head

"Are not five sparrows sold for two pennies? And not one of them is forgotten before God. Why even the hairs of your head are all numbered. Fear not; you are of more value than many sparrows" - Luke 12:6–7

The word 'No' has always had a negative reputation, but it seems to have gained a new level of notoriety in recent years. I've entered the global trillion-dollar parenting industry (do we need sound machines? I don't know, but I have two) and all the well-meaning (often conflicting) advice it entails. One of the trending topics these days is to limit negative language when it comes to parenting infants or toddlers, specifically to avoid saying "no" and instead promote positive language such as "why not this instead?". I understand the benefits, but I also understand that mommy sometimes needs a pot of coffee before she can stretch out a quick 'no' into a positive phrase, and that is just the way things are.

Daughter, I have one more story to share from this season of my life when I was a young woman looking to forge my path in my workplace, and how it was only later I realized that it was a loving No, covered in a father's protection. They say God always answers our prayer, usually with a yes, no, or not yet. This was one of the first times I had received a devastating no, and it is now one of the answers from Him that I am most thankful for in life because I know that as a Father, He knew what was best for me, even though I did not.

At that moment, though, the no was a hard pill to swallow. I was early in my career, and the world was my oyster. As my current stint as a graduate was coming to an end, it was time to make some moves at work and look for a permanent department to work in with my employer. I had a strong desire to work in the Business Development team, but at my level of seniority (or lack thereof), there were no analyst positions in the team in question, as the role typically requires experience and maturity. A few trusted people in the team I spoke to advised me to do something else and then try again in the future. I didn't even bother praying to God about it. What was the point of asking for something that didn't exist, even though it was one of my deepest desires? Instead, I looked around and applied to another position that seemed reasonably interesting and one which had a final shortlist of two applicants, including myself. The odds were good. By then, I was back in church, full of faith and on fire for God. I just knew He would give me this position because it was the best one out there, as far as I could see, and He had not failed me in the past.

And then came the rejection.

I couldn't understand it and had been so sure I would get this role. I was crushed and embarrassed because my successor had already come into my current team, and I had to move desks to another area - stuck in 'limbo.' Disappointed but undeterred, I applied for another role in London, UK. I was excited about a new adventure, even though the position was far from what I wanted to do. I had just met my husband-to-be but though I would be disappointed to part ways as we were starting our relationship, it would not have warranted giving up an international move. I had a great interview, but I did not hear back for weeks, if not months. This was unusual as you typically hear back within two weeks. What was going on? Has God forgotten me?

One day, out of the blue, my manager pulled me into a meeting room; as I walked in with trepidation, wondering what bad news could await me now, I sat down and braced myself. She went on to inform me that there was a newly created position in the Business Development team at my level of seniority, one that didn't exist previously. She said that she was aware of my application to London, and even though the manager in London wanted to hire me, Human Resources had asked to slow down the process with London because they knew this position was coming up. It was listed as my aspired top choice. I was elated, nervous, and probably more scared about getting the job than not getting it, but I was certainly not one to let go of the opportunity of a lifetime. Within a few months, I was starting in my new team, one that, for the next eight years, will mold, grow, challenge, and stretch me in ways that someone of my age and background could only hope for. It also meant that I stuck around in Singapore, resulting in the start of a decade-long (and counting!) relationship between my husband and me, and it has opened up life to me in a way that I never even imagined. Years later, when I would look to move to Houston with my husband, the leadership of that team would support me and move mountains to enable me to move to Texas even during a period of lay-offs.

"Take delight in the LORD, and he will give you the desires of your heart." - Psalm 37:4

With time, I would appreciate what happened there a bit better. When my husband and I discovered I was pregnant with my first daughter, we opened a savings account for our yet-unborn daughter. We wanted to ensure that she had something set aside for her education when she came of age. I believe we even managed to disagree on our approach to university (one in favor of this wise choice and the other absurdly against) before she had even lifted her head during tummy time. Such was the ardor with which we both violently agreed on wanting to support what was best for her. As Yoda might put it, 'Strong, our love was.' Even in the year leading up to even trying to get pregnant, I started taking prenatal vitamins, caught up on my chicken pox vaccine (which I never received as a child), and changed my lifestyle to make sure that I could prepare my body to be the best possible host environment for her when she arrives. When she was but an embryo at the age of three weeks, I started eating breakfast, something I usually skipped favoring a cup of coffee instead. When we listened to her heartbeat at seven weeks, we were making plans for a nursery. For the next few weeks and months, I was planning for everything we would need to have at home to meet her every need, not just for her first few weeks of life but the first months or years. While I was investing in developmental toys, my husband kept buying baby Jordans (second-hand, thank goodness!), shoes that she will not even wear for years to come yet, but even I could not help but think of how cute they were.

And if I, in my limited human way, loved our daughter so much as to plan for her future which has not yet materialized, how much more would our God in heaven think of and prepare good things for us? The Bible says that He cares about the details in our lives so much that He even knows the number of hairs on our heads! That does not sound like a Father who is uninterested in the things that matter to us. I believe that it is a Father who wants us to live full, thriving lives full of passion and energy, pursuing the dreams that He has placed in our hearts and fully using the gifts He has given us.

How the parent gently guides the child through the day, giving food when the child needs it, giving shelter and comfort that the child is not even aware it needs, even working out play and exercises before the child can even walk, to provide them with the opportunity to develop. The child cries out with wants and desires, yes, but it is the parent who directs and answers according to what the child needs. Much in the same way, I find it profoundly peace-giving to know that our Father does not just sit passively waiting for our requests, to grant or deny according to His will; no, He is always working for our Good, even when we do not know what that is; "And we know that in all things God works for the good of those who love Him, who have been called according to His purpose" (Romans 8:28). Understandably, my prayers have evolved from 'Father, grant me this one thing' to 'Father, I want this, but you know what is for my good much more than I ever could, and so I ask that your will, which I know if for my Good, be done in my life'. In this way, I can say that every single prayer of mine has been, and will be, answered in the way I hoped they would be.

wife

Nihara Guruge

3. nuptiae

It took a decade of being together, including five years of marriage, before I felt the impulsive urge to be romantic in public and grab my husband's hand as we strolled through a mall. It was always something my husband initiated, especially back when we were dating, often met with an awkward stumble on my part, followed by a laser focus on how synchronized we were in our footsteps, with my conservative South-Asian upbringing causing me acid-reflux at any forms of public displays of affection. He would always roll his eyes at me or sometimes call me out, having no such qualms after being raised in the USA. In this instance, I was reminiscing about us and feeling a little romantic, so I grabbed his hand. He immediately snatched his hand back, literally jumped away from me, and for added effect, furiously whispered, '*We can't!*' In my state of daydreaming and reminiscing, I had completely forgotten that at the very moment I had chosen to be romantic, we were strolling through a mall in the Middle East, where such affections were not on display publicly. If failure was my goal, my timing was nothing, if not excellent. We had a good giggle over the whole thing.

It was hard to believe that we were laughing like we were dating again in that aggressively air-conditioned mall when only a few months before I was sitting in my living room, completely distraught, frustrated, and wanting to give up.

My mind was thrown back to another hot, humid place five years ago, a continent away. A beautiful day in Galle Fort, Sri Lanka, where two young(er) optimists, brimming with possibility, had decided to make a go at it together, so confident in themselves, each other, and their future that they dared to make a covenant union before God. The choir was singing, and the music echoed through the old walls of the historic church, so wonderfully decorated with even the cracks in the stone emanating beauty, as I walked down the aisle. Unbeknownst to us, one of our friends from Singapore had already fainted from heat exhaustion. I was on the brink of crossing over from bridal glow to bridal showers of sweat as the veil over my face prevented even a hint of a breeze from reaching my flushed cheeks. I noticed that my husband was already sweating in his three-piece suit, though likely unaware of the fact as he stood there at the altar, looking serious but with glistening eyes. Later, my husband would ask me what thoughts were going on in my mind as I walked down the aisle to this union. I had to change the subject to prevent myself from confessing that everything up until the veil was lifted, giving me a breath of cool air, was a tropical haze and not a romantic one.

Once the death-inducing veil was removed, however, I was fully present in that moment, which would be one of the most significant moments in my life. Our hearts were full of love for God, who had done unimaginable things, closed and opened doors, and maneuvered impossible odds to make this girl from Sri Lanka and this boy from Texas meet in Singapore, fall in love, and decide to commit their relationship to God and were now entering into a union. At that moment, I know without a doubt that we both could not have put to words the absolute conviction with which we believed that God had brought us together for his purpose. I imagine cold feet was something made up by Hollywood because I had zero doubts about the decision we had made to spend our lives together. God was present as we raised our hands in praise and worship, with our friends and family assembled from as far and wide as the USA, Australia, UK, and Singapore. Our hearts were full of hope for the future and conviction as we said our vows to each other.

The pastor, somewhat predictably, read out Corinthians 13; *"Love is patient, love is kind. It does not envy, it does not boast, it is not proud. It does not dishonor others, it is not self-seeking, it is not easily angered, it keeps no record of wrongs...."* I promised to cherish and honor my husband. The priest got to the part about submitting to my husband, and approximately one-half of the congregation laughed, much to my chagrin. Granted, it was justified. No one who knew up until that point could imagine me submitting to my spouse meekly. It was a humorous, cute moment, a good story to be recited later, but an ominous forewarning of things to come. One of the in-vogue things these days is writing letters to your future self. If I could do the reverse, I would have visited my thirty-year-old self then, smacked the smirk off her face, and said, "Look sharp, you are in for a rude awakening."

Later I would realize how ill-prepared I was for marriage and how over-confident we both were in what preparation we had engaged in. The church we attended in Singapore was known for the absolute excellence of their marriage preparation series. It is several months of weekend classes followed by up to six months of one-on-one counseling with a senior pastor, with customized online personality compatibility test reports issued to the couple before even an engagement is endorsed. It is marriage preparation in the true sense whereby if, at the end of the one year, it is deemed that you are either incompatible or not yet ready for the life-long commitment that is marriage, the pastors would not provide support for the union. This is to underscore the importance and permanence of the marriage union and to emphasize further that any pastor who stands at the altar facilitating this holy union is doing so with a clear conscience in the belief of the lifelong success of the union.

My husband and I had been through this journey and found no areas of concern with our finances (we agreed on tithing, giving, and saving), children (my husband was okay with or without, and I leaned heavily towards without), and other typical areas of concern covered over the course. We were issued a report noting that we were a "Vitalized couple," that being a couple that tends to have the highest Positive Couple Agreement scores across most of the categories with maybe some work to do in conflict management, which we brushed aside (oh how humorous that seems to me now). The apparent lack of incompatibility issues, our high individual propensity to want to succeed at all that we do, and our faith had us both at that altar somewhat confident that "pfft, we got this!".

With the benefit of hindsight, I realize now how little we 'got' this. Nothing can drive that home harder than hearing the words, *"that's it, I'm done,"* being thrown around, even if not in sincerity, then at least as a symbol of a complete disconnect, a mere four years later.

Upon reflection, I have realized that what I expected of marriage was a mish-mash of popular media (romantic comedies should be boycotted, in my opinion), our memories of our parents' marriages (bearing in mind that as children, we do tend to gloss over anything that doesn't affect us directly) which for the most part we were sheltered from, or had no memory of. I don't care if you are the world's foremost couple's counselor, marriage therapist, psychologist, or marriage guru (does such a thing exist?) or read every book on marriage. Until you are married, you do not truly know what marriage entails. I certainly didn't. And I had little understanding of marriage other than the bit about having to submit to my husband, which didn't sit well with me.

Daughter, this is why I am writing you this letter, hoping that you may read it and reflect on it *before* you embark on one of your life's greatest and most challenging adventures, *marriage.* I will share the rollercoaster I have been on so far, the hurt, the pain, and the hope and joy on the other side. I will try to set aside my pride and shame and share all it took from me to submit to God. But most of all, if nothing else, remember this; let this be an awakening to the greatness of the undertaking and effort required to keep a marriage rooted and afloat through the difficult times, an endeavor whose success or failure, I believe, will require a partner equally worthy and up to the task. So, choose well, my daughter, and choose wisely. You must be able to imagine or expect your chosen life partner to be with you on the battlefield, protecting your marriage against all that seeks to tear it down. I guarantee you that it will require all hands on deck at times because you can rest assured the enemy will not be pulling their punches.

So how did we go from that hot, blissful day in that church in Sri Lanka to the frigid, biting winter within the four walls of what we called home? The short answer is probably four years of taking each other for granted. The long answer looks more like a less-than-fun version of the popular game, or as I call it, the wheel of misfortune.

Perhaps it was the pregnancy, fully experienced during the start and peak of COVID-19, isolating me from all loved ones I always assumed would be a part of such an experience, with travel restrictions preventing even my mother from being there to make me a hot meal, or guide me through labor. This new reality of isolation during the COVID-19 pandemic led to (however unconsciously) ever-increased expectations of my husband to not only be partner and husband but play the role of mother, sister, friend, and doula. I find it unsurprising that instead of the expected baby boom predicted by experts, the pandemic quarantine is rumored to have resulted in a boom in divorces.

Perhaps it was the birth of our daughter, whom we love so much but whose presence forever changed the dynamic of our marriage. Certainly, I am guilty of completely falling in love with my daughter and fully embracing this new role of Mother. I never envisioned for myself or dreamed that I would be good at it, to the extent that all other areas and interests in my life seemed to shrink to oblivion. The best way I can describe it is as if one light switched on, while all the other lights in all the other rooms just switched off. It would be many months before some of those lights would start to flicker back on.

Perhaps it was due to the questionnaire that I had to fill out at the pediatrician's office during every visit post-birth. The questions always indicated that everything was A-OK. I was not considering harming myself or my baby, nor did I feel detached and unemotional about her or her life. And yet, it was one of the loneliest periods of my life where I could not find a moment alone to myself and yet felt the weight of being alone crushing me daily.

My maternity leave was a blessing and looking back on that time now, I am grateful. I worked for a wonderful European multinational that took supportive family leave policies seriously. This meant I could have up to four months of paid leave and up to another twelve months unpaid, no questions asked. I decided to take six months off in total. But after the first two months, my husband's paternity leave ended, and he returned to work while I stayed home. That was when the cracks began to appear on the wall. I had always thrived on intellectual challenges, high-pressure situations, and impossible deliverables and was naturally an extrovert. It was unsurprising, therefore, that as much as I enjoyed the rest and time with my daughter (and I would have done anything to make sure she would spend her early months and years at home being taken care of by a caregiver), after a few months I started to crack. When I was ready to go back to work, I would swear that my husband could not even breathe without irritating me. Looking back now, I can discern that it had less to do with whether or not he could anticipate diaper needs ahead of time and more to do with my frustrations of being cooped up.

I would often say that pandemic aside, 2020 was a good year for us, highlighted by the birth of our daughter. Equally, 2021 felt like the year from hell, or at least an apocalyptic novel, as a winter storm hit us early on in the year in Houston, Texas, in February, while I was still on maternity leave. Testament to how unprepared the State is for such sudden climate events can be seen no further than how all the houses were designed with no insulation.

Maybe even open vents to let the hot air out during summer. To top it off, most of the power grid was designed around temperatures not falling below zero Celsius, which meant that the beautiful morning of snow was followed by no power (including heating) and no water for too many houses for almost a week. While we only lost water, we were saddled with a four-month-old baby on formula (and therefore needed filtered water) as first-time parents, petrified, wondering if we could take care of her as the roads iced up and supplies ran dry.

I recall a moment early in the week, when we realized we had to shut off the water pipes to prevent them from freezing and bursting, with no regret as no water was coming through anyway, I calculated that we had four toilet flushes in our bathrooms in the house. Unfortunately, neither of us had the foresight to fill a bathtub with water when the initial warnings came. I did some careful mental math (which I never hope to do again) and planned how we could stretch usage for as long as possible. Feeling somewhat prepared, I recall being in the kitchen with my daughter when I suddenly heard the tell-tale sound of a toilet flushing, the last sound I wanted to hear at that moment. I ran down, my anger building with each step I took down the stairs to confront my sheepish-looking husband, who shrugged and said, 'I just did it without thinking'. With the benefit of hindsight, it seems like such a small thing now, but at that moment, I reckon there was no demon in hell who felt as much fury as I did. But many baby wipes and bottles of water which were later brought over by our friends from church over icy roads; this storm (both the actual winter storm and the one in my mind) also passed.

The icing on the cake was the corporate restructuring at our company, much like all other companies and industries in response to COVID-19, which meant that I was technically at risk of being laid off for most of the year.

All of this took place within less than a year.

It still took me by surprise, perhaps because of how great of a start we had in our relationship, to wake up one day and realize that the temperature inside the home has dropped a few degrees below the cold weather outside the house.

I suppose I should not have been shocked. For months, I had been in survival mode, rolling with the punches, jumping from one crisis to the next, fully confident of my ability to deal with whatever was thrown at me. Everyone forewarned me that when a baby enters the mix, even without a pandemic, it is so important to prioritize time with each other to maintain the relationship, but this was the furthest thing from my mind, perhaps not even on the list at all. How could it be when it felt like I was going from one day to the next, treading water, juggling so many balls, feeling as though one mistake, one misstep, could catapult me into dropping them all? Our pre-marital training and the wisdom of those who came before us prepared us for conflict regarding finances, disagreements about children or care for loved ones, or approach to working or child-rearing. But nothing had prepared me for the slow decay that starts to set in when one starts to treat one's partner as nothing more than a project team member whose sole responsibility is to fulfill their share of the tasks at hand or with the added responsibility of meeting all your needs and making you happy.

Daughter, before I go any further, I must state that I am not interested in detailing how much we struggled in this season or the inevitable irritability, conflicts, or impatience. No, these letters are only about one relationship, which is the one between Jesus and me. I have learned that our struggle is not unique or uncommon. So be prepared so you may wisely avoid the path well-trodden. After all, one does not build a roof over their house because they expect clear skies.

Before you start to wonder, yes, through all this, I *did* pray. I prayed for a speedy resolution of repairs. I prayed for provision and for open doors. I prayed for protection against what felt like attack after attack by the enemy.

But if I was being honest, I must admit that I did not pray for patience. I did not pray for wisdom, to understand if there was a purpose behind this, which He was trying to tell me. I did not pray for peace in all circumstances. I prayed only for my circumstances to change so that I could have peace. I did not pray for grace toward myself or my husband.

Instead of thanking God that He has equipped me to deal with any crisis, that He has given us the resources to see this through, that He created me with the ability to handle multiple things at the same time, compartmentalize, ruthlessly organize and keep many balls juggling in the air, I chose to be critical. I felt resentful that I had to carry so much in the first place. I prayed instead for my husband to 'see things my way,' which is just another way of hoping that he has the same personality characteristics as me so that we will have perfect harmony when we solve problems or take care of our daughter. His unique strengths were of lesser interest to me, only that he aligned with my views.

Daughter, when you place your impossible expectations on others, willing them to change into your idealized standards instead of who God made them to be in the first place, there is only one likely outcome; failure and disappointment. It was unsurprising then that I was filled with bitterness and resentment by the tail end of this crisis.

The thing about self-righteousness is that it is lonely at the top. It's also not a great vantage point to see. Have you ever sat in the nose-bleed section at a basketball game or court-side? Guess which one is better? Court-side, of course! That is where you can see how tall the players are, get a whiff of game-time aromas of sweat and popcorn, and have to leave early if you want to get out of the parking lot within a decent amount of time.

But that was not where I was. I was sitting on my self-erected pedestal, blind to all my husband did daily and only seeing what he didn't do. He didn't do this, and he didn't do that. The list goes on and on. My list did not include how he would religiously take out the trash every day. Or bought groceries whenever I asked or how he shared equally in bath time and bedtime when it came to my daughter, how he would let me sleep in for an hour in the morning on weekends, picking up my daughter when she woke up, how he makes an effort to bond with my family and cares for their wellbeing, how he would never say no to someone who asked him for help or to serve, how he was generous with his giving. How he so freely gave of his time and energy to anyone who needed it. That list, too, goes on and on. It's just taken for granted, ironically, in the same way that I complained that I am taken for granted.

Marriage aside, how often are we guilty of this in *all* our relationships? I am quick to forgive my mistakes and shortcomings but expect so much more from others. Perhaps that is why Jesus had to specifically ask us, *"Why do you look at the speck of sawdust in your brother's eye and pay no attention to the plank in your own eye? "(*Matthew 7:3).

As my resentment grew, fueled by the stress I was too arrogant to acknowledge that I was under (even as my hair started to fall out more and more, well past the usual postpartum hair loss period), patience levels dropped, tones became curter and more accusatory, love banks started to run low. Were we surviving, or were we happy? If not to make me happy, what is even the purpose of marriage in the first place?

"Though one may be overpowered, two can defend themselves. A cord of three strands is not quickly broken." - Ecclesiastes 4:12

To anyone looking to answer this question, I would direct you towards the Bible first and foremost, supplemented by a wonderful book called *Sacred Marriage* by Gary Thomas, which sought to answer the question, "What if God designed marriage to make us Holy more than to make us happy"? I encourage anyone, married or contemplating marriage, to read this book which brings such a mindset of eternity into marriage. I ordered a copy, and thanks to Amazon, I had the book in my hand by 10 pm that night. That is very typical behavior on my part; there isn't a problem on earth that can't be solved by reading a book about it. I wasn't quite praying with the right intent in my heart, but I *was* asking for help, and my prayer was heard in heaven. Daughter, remember how I encouraged you earlier to do your best to choose someone who will be an equal on the battlefield? What happened the next day makes me laugh to this day. As I was praying and seeking a path forward, my husband had been doing the same. As a result, he showed up with two copies of *Sacred Marriage* the next day, proposing that we read it together as a devotional (we had three copies in total till we gave it away to another couple). I believe that God led us to this thought together and that He continues to help us and guard our marriage, even as we seek him more and more. Daughter, we are not fighting alone. If we are fortunate, our husbands will be fighting alongside us. But even if they are not, God fights for us.

Nihara Guruge

4. refined

"This third I will put into the fire; I will refine them like silver and test them like gold. They will call on my name and I will answer them; I will say, 'They are my people,' and they will say, 'The Lord is our God.'" - Zechariah 13:9

Every time I take away a touch-screen phone from my daughter, who keeps finding ways to get her hands on them despite our best efforts to hide them from her, I am met with ear-splitting howling and wailing. If I'm extra lucky, she will throw herself around, appearing to hurt herself, just to scare me into giving her back what she wants. The latter was more amusing than concerning as my daughter just had such a good sense of self-preservation from a young age that while she threw herself down on the floor, she would carefully lower her head so as not to hit it hard on the floor. The result was a comical half-sit-up that we observed her attempting to complete while crying and looking despondent. Nonetheless, it never changed my mind because I do not believe the phone is beneficial for her and perhaps even harmful, so out of my love for her, I would allow her to feel that loss in the hope that one day she will understand, and maybe even love me for it. Over time the tantrums have become shorter and shorter to the extent that now, she would point at it and look at me hopefully, seeking permission, before picking up the phone, as she knows she is not supposed to have it.

My God is an even more loving Father, who I believe allowed certain events to unfold in my life to test and reveal strongholds that I did not even know were a part of my life.

We all probably remember setting fire to something in physics class in middle or high school, hopefully intentionally and under constant supervision. I've always been fascinated by the chemical composition of entities, whether it is organic, like humans, or inorganic, such as various metals and substances in this world. Take, for example, metals that look broadly similar, but when inspected further, you realize how differently the atoms are bonded together. This uniqueness allows us to melt stainless steel at 1510 degrees Celsius but requires a whopping 3400 degrees Celsius to melt tungsten. As a result, we all have tungsten in our homes as this resistance to heat makes it ideal to be used as a filament in lightbulbs.

I think people are not so very different. At one point in my life, I was so fascinated by the differences in our personalities that I spent a good chunk of my weekends and personal funds to take various personality profiling courses, with the hope that I could maybe understand why communication with some people often seemed like water rolling off a duck's back, while with others it felt like a pairing of apple pie with a scoop of ice cream. I received a good return on investment as I concluded the courses with a confirmation of my original hypothesis, which is that we are all so very differently made (thankfully with a few tools to navigate these differences), so at least I can rest a bit easier when I feel misunderstood.

But much like metals, which require different amounts of energy to break apart the chemical composition, I think we have different 're-making' points. I've faced and overcome many obstacles in my life, which in itself sounds like a great notion, but what it meant in my journey as a Christian woman of faith was that I was all too comfortable and confident in my ability to navigate anything that life throws at me, whether it is a lost passport while traveling or an extensive home renovation project. It stands to reason that God would need to throw a lot more heat at me to get my attention. Certainly, a lot more heat than that if I am to be melted down and made into something better.

We live in a world that tells us daily to listen to our hearts. That self-care is important, a notion I believe only to the extent that it was reflected in how Jesus took care of himself with rest, meditation, and prayer, while still living a self-sacrificial life. Unfortunately, self-care has become about what makes you feel happy, which puts your emotions in the driving seat, the modern-day equivalent of letting your drunk grandpa with cataracts drive the car. Emotions themselves aren't necessarily evil. How can they be when even God and Jesus are shown to have emotions in the Bible, and we were made in God's image? But I have often found that my emotions, when unchecked or uncontrolled, have kicked me into a spiral of negativity, feeling as though there was no way forward because I did not feel happy.

Jesus taught us, "Love the Lord your God with all your heart and with all your soul and with all your strength and with all your mind" in Luke 10:27. I find this so profound because we always presuppose that love is a matter of the heart, but God says that equally there is a role for the mind and your body (our actions) to play. Why did He feel the need to call out the mind? Was it because, without the mind, the heart can be led astray? And without the heart, the mind can be cold and cruel?

Regardless, I have come to believe that the health of a marriage is forged or broken in the Mordor of Marriage- the mind (I apologize for the Lord of the Rings reference- I'm a fan!). It is where we fall in love with our spouse and, in those early days, spend many hours or days thinking of how amazing they are, daydreaming of our future, and allowing our thoughts to dwell on all their great qualities. It is also the same place we spiral into, ending up in a pit of despair, believing that nothing can improve our current circumstances and that it is better to give up and walk away.

I don't know if you associate the heart and mind with very different things like me. The mind is for intellectual pursuits, even a higher understanding of God and the natural and supernatural laws. The heart is for emotions and feelings, dreams and desires. Of course, we all know that when it comes to the actual organs, we mean the brain for all things, but you get my gist. But here was God telling me to love Him with all my mind. It didn't seem like a logical place to start re-building my long list of issues in the relationship, but that is where God directed me to slowly begin.

"We demolish arguments and every pretension that sets itself up against the knowledge of God, and we take captive every thought to make it obedient to Christ." -2 Corinthians 10:5

Captive? Demolish? Obedient? Sounds like war to me. And frankly, it sounds exhausting. But it is war. There are always forces surrounding us that would love nothing better than to tear apart a marriage, break down the threefold cord and leave its scars for generations to come. What better way to attempt to derail the purpose of two individuals, a couple, or their children than to entangle all parties in the aftermath of a painful divorce? If your adversary is at war, you can't exactly take the passive approach. War it is then, and we start with the mind. I didn't know how to address the heart matters; emotions felt like something that 'happened' to me. But here, as a step in the refining process, God showed me the first thing we needed to work on- my thoughts.

It was a baby step, but the next time I started to get a hint of mild irritation at some act of thoughtlessness or even a hurtful remark, I decided to employ my mind, which is usually reserved for the benefit of my employer, and set to work. Was what I was feeling true? Was what I was thinking biblically true? What exactly did the *Bible* say about my husband, the real source of truth, and not my emotions? Or any person who I was struggling to have a relationship with?

I set out to find promises about our identity revealed in the Bible, characteristics that I usually employ to affirm and edify myself, and tested it out on my husband's identity instead.

- He has been fearfully and wonderfully created (Psalm 139:14)

- He has been created in God's image (Genesis 1:27)

- He has been knitted together in his mother's womb by God himself (Psalm 139:13)

- God has known him before he was born (Jeremiah 1:5)

- He is precious and honored in God's sight (Isaiah 43:4)

- He is a child of God (Romans 8:17)

As I began to meditate on these thoughts over and over (and not on what my husband said to me or did or did not do), I began to glimpse what it meant to take my thoughts captive. I also began to understand the battlefield references; it felt like a wrestling match was going on for my thoughts. Even as I kept elevating my thoughts, there were voices whispering negativity and doubts, reminding me of past or current hurts and encouraging me to dwell on his imperfections. If I could imagine a boardroom full of guardian angels, I could equally imagine ugly winged creatures whispering their poisonous words hoping something would stick.

What does it mean to see my husband through God's eyes and not my own? Looking at him through my eyes, I see imperfections. Through God's eyes, I can see creation in all its glory.

One of my favorite authors is Agatha Christie, one of the absolute greats of crime fiction, in my opinion. As a fiction writer, one of her notable quotes was, '*imagination is a good servant and a bad master.*' I can't help but think of how humorously this plays out in relationships sometimes. I can see my husband quiet and imagine that he is sulking, then decide to put two and two together and conclude that he must be upset at that thing I said and did earlier or was not appropriately grateful for something I was doing or saying at the moment. This leads to resentment on my part as I work myself up into a huff, thinking he has no right to be upset as surely, I should be the one who should be upset at this *other* thing he did at five o'clock the night before and so on. And all the while, the poor man has been wondering if he will get to go to the gym or if he will be forced to run outside in the heat because of his schedule! This an excellent illustration of another easy area where we can employ our otherwise brilliant and logical minds.

What else could I do with my mind? I insisted that we seek a Christian counselor, a wonderful professional recommended by our pastor. However, I was slightly miffed when he told me during one of the sessions, 'you *are* a bit intense,' which frankly sounded like common feedback received by women who weren't afraid to have a strong opinion. Despite our grasp of the English language, it seemed like we left every conversation with each other feeling like one or both of us could not translate our thoughts effectively. With his help, we were able to decode some of the communications going back and forth. If nothing else, I will always recommend good Christian counseling and mediation for any struggling relationship, even as a proactive measure. I also ordered every book I could find on restoring marriages and read most of them faithfully.

The counseling helped, but we could never quite go back to what we were before. I couldn't help but wonder, were the days of giggling and joy already behind us? It wasn't long before old, unresolved issues resurfaced again.

One desperate evening, I sat in my living room, alone and distraught. For lack of anything else I could think of to do to make myself feel better, I was singing along to the lyrics of 'Shout to the Lord' by Darlene Joyce Zschech. The song was on a loop, articulating something that I was too anguished to put into words, as is often the case when we worship through our pain.

The desperation to restore a relationship has done what no prayer or concern for financial provision, career aspiration, or prayer for salvation for a loved one has done before. As much faith as I had, I was a problem solver. Therefore, my prayer to God was followed by a solid action plan (or sometimes vice versa) which I was able to put into action to drive issues to resolution. But this time, it was different. This was a heart issue, one I felt wholly unqualified to repair. All I could do was say, 'God, please help me'.

"If you remain in me and my words remain in you, ask whatever you wish, and it will be done for you." -John 15:7

I talk a lot, so I can probably do much more to listen. I did listen at this moment, as I was desperate for an answer. I suddenly felt, heard, and sensed what I needed to do. I was about to be given a dose of hope. I scrambled for a piece of paper and started writing down the following.

Time of writing: October 21, 2021
My marriage has been fully restored. Our friendship is stronger than ever, and there is an overabundance of love and respect. It feels like we are dating again. We can't wait to speak with, and spend time with each other. We are expecting our second child, a girl, a sister to our daughter.

As for my career, I will have great hours, which will allow for much rest and a smooth pregnancy. I received a fantastic opportunity to further my talents and dreams. The door opened so unexpectedly and clearly that I knew it was from God. He is Good, and all good things are from him, given at the right time. My family was closer and is very much a part of our life, and will be helping with our baby and Liel when she is born.

We lack nothing.

The last time I wrote down something like this, I was goal-setting at the age of sixteen. Except for the Ferrari (which seems like an exciting goal when you are a teenager, but as an adult gave me no confidence as something that can keep this new driver safe on the Texas highways), the rest of the list had come true. There is power in words. Writing down something like this was to throw a gauntlet down, a challenge to the very existence of my faith like a shout from the mountaintop. I felt strongly that I had to declare what is to be rather than what is. As the words got penned, I felt a great sense of relief and hope. I was thrown a lifeline to keep going in faith. It was with God now as a prayer and a declaration of faith. It was out of the physical realm that we can see and touch and in the spiritual realm where things can come to be. I slept well that night.

I didn't stop there, worried that it was again another emotional response. I went back to my declaration several times over the next few weeks, testing if it was in line with biblical truths and praying. Was I asking my husband to change so I could treat him better? Was I asking him to become more like me so we could get along swimmingly? I think the answer is No. I felt more confident in my declaration.

A sidebar on that last point, because it is a tempting prayer to make, and I will be the first to raise my hand to say I have done it too. I can ask my husband (or anyone I was struggling with) to change to be someone I view as 'perfect' - sure. But does that help me in eternity when I am standing alone in front of God? I won't have anyone next to me to say, 'hey God, remember that time I was irritable and snarky? Well, if only he had done what he said he would, it wouldn't have happened'. No, I think the stark reality of facing judgment alone is a constant reminder that we can only control ourselves and our reactions and will ultimately be accountable for our thoughts, words, and actions regardless of the circumstances that led to them. This is both a terrifying thought and a liberating one. Terrifying for the weight of accountability it places on us. Liberating as we can be set entirely free of all that is around us, and only responsible for our actions and thoughts and words, and none others. For that same reason, I am intentionally not focusing on my husband, his actions, or his journey in this letter. We need to focus on what we control, and that is ourselves.

And one thing I could do, which I did in the following days, weeks, and months was to bury myself in the Word of God, looking directly to the source for a way forward. It was then that I came across this passage;

"Blessed are all who fear the Lord, who walk in obedience to him. You will eat the fruit of your labor; blessings and prosperity will be yours. Your wife will be like a fruitful vine within your house; your children will be like olive shoots around your table. Yes, this will be the blessing for the man who fears the Lord." - Psalm 128:1-4

This verse gave me a sense of overwhelming peace. A wife who is like a fruitful wine? Children like olive shoots? If nothing else, it gives me a sense of transcending peace to visualize this living room; full of peace, blessings, and love. I was determined to have this peace in my household and do whatever it takes to bring that peace into my life and our home, if not for my sake, then certainly for my daughter's sake. I began to pray desperately for peace, both in the house and within me. With determination, I dove into the Bible, seeking, wanting, searching for an answer that I knew would be there. Some guidelines that I would need to implement. Something that I could do! I started re-reading the Gospels, looking for a teaching, miracle, or parable that might be the lighthouse that could direct me. Jesus said He was 'the way, the truth, and the light,' meaning He would be able to provide what I was looking for.

I was not wrong. Eventually, I re-read what I would admit is one of my least favorite teachings of Jesus, not because it is not beautiful or meaningful, but because it always felt like an impossible standard to uphold for myself. The passage is called 'The Beatitudes.'

"Blessed are the poor in spirit, for theirs is the kingdom of heaven. Blessed are those who mourn, for they will be comforted. Blessed are the meek, for they will inherit the earth. Blessed are those who hunger and thirst for righteousness, for they will be filled. Blessed are the merciful, for they will be shown mercy. Blessed are the pure in heart, for they will see God.

Blessed are the peacemakers, for they will be called children of God. Blessed are those who are persecuted because of righteousness, for theirs is the kingdom of heaven. Blessed are you when people insult you, persecute you and falsely say all kinds of evil against you because of me. Rejoice and be glad, because great is your reward in heaven, for in the same way they persecuted the prophets who were before you" - Matthew 5: 3-12

I started to scribble down my 'revelations' in the margins of my Bible. Poor in spirit? I need much more humility and less pride than I had been exhibiting. Was I so great and my husband so bad? Am I so perfect with no faults of my own? Did Jesus not need to die for my sins too? The answer was clearly no, no, and yes, he did. Those who mourn? How soft was my heart? I was often moved to compassion by the poor, downtrodden, marginalized, orphans, and widows. But was I equally softhearted towards my husband? Shouldn't I be even more softhearted towards the person who is my life partner than I was to strangers on the street? Blessed are the meek? I suppose this is not the person with the rapid-fire replies to accusations but the one who holds their tongue. The one who can follow. The one who can submit. Just like Jesus did to his enemies.

How merciful am I in my marriage towards my spouse? Do I forgive and forget easily? Or do I keep score, unable to move on from offenses? And most of all, the peacemakers. Not the debaters, the fighters, the retaliators. But the forebearers, forgivers, and active restorers. The first to swallow their pride in a fight and break a frigid silence, the first to apologize, the first to acknowledge their part in the issue, the first to say, 'I love you, and I value our relationship and if something is not working for you, let's change it'. Above all, I felt Jesus gently gave me a template to follow in all things. And He didn't just say what we should do but will go on to show us through going to his death, like a lamb to the slaughter, even though He could have commanded the armies in heaven to storm Jerusalem and set him free.

And so, this is what I had to do to generate a positive change in my marriage. I had a roadmap for my thoughts, and now I had one for my actions. I spent hours diving into Paul's letters in the New Testament. I meditated on his plight, his deep misfortune in life, and how He still attained an unfathomable peace, despite his circumstances, his hope firmly set on eternity, life after death where real joy can be found. I comforted myself in the thought that this life with all its challenges is short and temporary, but I have hope for true joy in heaven one day when this life is past.

And so, I was armed two-fold; One, using my effort and strength to follow the ideal template Jesus set for us in his teachings and life; to be an ideal Christ-follower and, therefore, wife. And two, a notion that no matter the outcome, I will endure on in the hope of joy in eternity.

Daughter, are you starting to see where I was setting myself up for failure? If you are, you are wiser than I was in that moment. I've come to realize that the beatitudes are a reflection or result of a pre-existing condition of the heart that *already was*; and not a checklist of things to do. I was still trying to use my own (well-meaning) strength and will. Our counselor once said that he tries not to give couples tools and tips for communication as he often find that they can be counterproductive without the underlying love connection being restored between the couple; they result in becoming new material for the couple to fight over. I laughed at the time, but I get it now. If my heart has not changed, all the tools in the world will only do so much.

Sure, the next time I was triggered, I was able to walk up the stairs muttering to myself, 'well, even Jesus was misunderstood in his time, unjustly accused and put to death,' and look to keep my mouth shut in an attempt to be meek. And the next time, and the next time. But, of course, it was not sustainable.

The only thing I was achieving was even more dissatisfaction and, if possible, a greater sense of self-righteousness and superiority. My expectations had not changed. If anything, I felt even more bitter and resentful, this time fueled by the belief that I was trying so hard to be better while he was seemingly not, again, a blatant mistruth led by my emotions. I still had the same expectations of him, and I had just tried to find a way to make peace with the fact that he may never meet them. I hadn't changed my heart or, more importantly, changed the lens through which I viewed my husband. Try as I might to change using my strength, I did not know how I could change. In other words, in my effort, I could not wake up and become a different person, the kind of person Jesus described in the beatitudes; any more than a wolf can become a sheep by choice. Sure, they can modify their behavior, which may even last a while. After all, we learn all kinds of things in life. Introverts learn to act like extroverts. Those who shun the spotlight can learn to speak in public. People who hate cooking (like me) can still learn to make pasta.

Only one person I knew was in the business of changing hearts, and he couldn't be found in the self-help section of the most popular bookstores. This time, I was so desperate for change, having failed using my strength, I was forced to look not into the teachings but at the teacher himself.

Nihara Guruge

5. justified

It was a typical, ordinary Sunday morning, and my husband and I were at our favorite spot in the church congregation, the second row from the stage, left aisle. But these are the ordinary moments that God chooses to reveal the extraordinary, convict, and restore if the subject is willing. As the music cascaded over me, the church, the service, and the worship team slipped out of my consciousness. My husband was beside me, occasionally bumping elbows as we swayed out of tune with each other. But he, too, was not in my thoughts. I was all alone, in front of God, in front of Jesus, who had paid such a heavy price to buy my life and my freedom in this life and for all eternity. And all I had to offer in return was myself. What else can I possibly offer back to God?

Truth be told, at that moment, I hated the offering. I hated every negative thought I had. I hated every harsh word that came out of my mouth in the heat of an argument. I hated my pride. I felt the weight of sin on my shoulders, threatening to crush me with shame. I had tried to be better and different, but I was tired of trying and failing.

> *"Two men went up to the temple to pray, one a Pharisee and the other a tax collector. The Pharisee stood by himself and prayed: 'God, I thank you that I am not like other people—robbers, evildoers, adulterers—or even like this tax collector. I fast twice a week and give a tenth of all I get.' But the tax collector stood at a distance. He would not even look up to heaven, but beat his breast and said, 'God, have mercy on me, a sinner.' I tell you that this man, rather than the other, went home justified before God. For all those who exalt themselves will be humbled, and those who humble themselves will be exalted."*
> *- Luke 18:10-14*

If anyone asks me what my purpose in life is, I will confidently be able to answer a truth that I discovered for myself a long time ago. My ultimate goal in this life is to live in such a way that when my time comes and I meet my Creator face to face, I can stand in front of Him and hear the treasured, precious words, *"well done, good and faithful servant."* Like the Pharisees, I had always thought I was doing 'okay.' After all, I try my best to serve, be generous, seek out needs in others, live biblically and honorably, and testify to God's goodness at every opportunity. But suddenly, in the face of my sin, I could not be sure anymore.

That day I stood at the altar, but in reality, far away, feeling more like that tax collector than I had ever felt. Unable to even lift my eyes up, so consumed with sin and shame that I felt unworthy to even ask for forgiveness, all I could say was, "I'm sorry."

Boy, when the Holy Spirit convicts, He sure does convict hard.

I have by no means led a perfect life, which means that being a Christian inevitably means that I was no stranger to the act of repentance. But while I had repented for my actions before, I was now in totally new and uncharted territory, wondering how to repent not just for my acts, thoughts, and words but for the very sin within me. To repent for the sinful person that I am. I felt something buried in me that I was desperate to claw out.

Shortly before this fateful morning, perhaps just a night or two, I had a vivid dream.

In my dream, I had driven to an event in my SUV and had pulled up to the entrance of the building. I was told that the event included a parking valet service whereby I just had to hand over my keys to the parking attendant, and he would park my car for me. Upon leaving the event, I would need to hand in my token to identify which car was mine, and the attendant would bring my car right up to the front of the door. The service was paid for by the event hosts and was free to be used by the guests. When it was time for me to leave, I decided to go in search of my car to retrieve it myself. As many familiar with valet service would know, the cars aren't always parked nearby, sometimes even as far as adjacent parking lots due to restrictions in space. I kept looking, and looking, and looking with the sun starting to beat down on me. I was hot, sweating, and fatigued. And still, I kept looking for my car. After a long while, faced with inevitable failure, I finally decided to return to the parking attendant and hand in my token. Within minutes, they retrieved my car. They knew where it was parked. After all, the service was bought and paid for.

I woke up sweating, feeling the fatigue in my muscles as if I had been running around in the hot sun looking for my car.

I rarely remember the details of my dreams, but this one was etched in my memory. As I stood there at the altar that morning, in my brokenness, I realized with humility that, in my pride, I had been trying to fix my marriage using my efforts. Worse, in my arrogance, I had been trying to change myself using my efforts as well. It was not unlike looking for a car that I had not parked.

Thankfully, someone much greater than me had already done that work. I just needed to take hold of it.

"For by one sacrifice, he has made perfect forever those who are being made holy. The Holy Spirit also testifies to us about this. First, he says: "This is the covenant I will make with them after that time, says the Lord.

I will put my laws in their hearts and write them on their minds." Then he adds: "Their sins and lawless acts I will remember no more."

And where these have been forgiven, sacrifice for sin is no longer necessary." - Hebrews 10:14-18

As I stood there at the altar, it wasn't condemnation or self-hatred that I settled on, although I swiftly moved past those states at the beginning. Those are tools of the enemy. It was the conviction of sin that only the Holy Spirit could reveal, followed by the burning hot truth that the price of our sin was already paid for, and we had only to come to the altar and claim freedom and forgiveness. I realized I didn't have to *try* so hard because I was already bought and paid for.

So why was I struggling alone with self-help books, personality profiles, and marriage tips? Those are wonderful resources, and I urge everyone to find out as much as possible about your spouse, children, colleagues, and loved ones. But they alone cannot help you renew a fading relationship. They alone cannot change your heart and mind. They alone cannot manipulate your relationships into manifesting the real change you desire. They alone could not make me into a different, better version of myself.

"Because the Lord disciplines the one he loves and chastens everyone he accepts as his son." - Hebrews 12:6

For the last eighteen months, it had felt like I was bombarded with one challenge after the other. The pandemic, the pregnancy, the loneliness of the two combined, postpartum recovery, job insecurity, a crumbling relationship, and a feeling of going through it alone. God needed my attention, yes, but to convict me to change in an area so deeply rooted in the very core of my DNA would take a tsunami, not a gentle breeze. In hindsight, I realized that some serious strongholds needed to be broken down before I entered the next season of my life, one that would be both an expansion, an increase, and a challenge that required much of me. It was time to graduate to a higher level. Like infants, level up from drinking milk, and move on to solid food. To fortify the tents and strengthen the foundations.

Daughter, I pray you start your journey much more pliable and softer than I was at that moment so that it would not take so many moments of crisis to turn to God in helpless surrender.

The Lord disciples those He loves, and I believe no tool in his toolkit is more effective than marriage. I have not come across another structure, social institution, or construct that can so effectively bring out the best and the worst in us to reveal our most selfless characteristics and deep selfishness. Certainly, no one will be able to hold up a mirror to you, revealing uncomfortable truths quite the way that your spouse can.

This is when we come to the fork in the road. If we were not followers of Christ, this is where the story ends. Perhaps we despair or eventually give up on our marriage, and maybe we spend the rest of our days wondering, 'What if I did things differently?' Or worse, settle for something less than the best life God has for us, a mediocre life of surviving instead of thriving. But I praise God because that is not the path for us believers of Christ.

The difference for us believers is that as I stood at the altar, with my head bowed and tears streaming down my cheeks, I felt the gentle, loving touch of Jesus wiping away the tears from my cheek. The consoling, almost fleeting sensation of my chin being nudged up. And then, the much more discernible awareness of a weight being lifted off my shoulders. All sins are forgiven. All burdens lifted onto another set of shoulders, straining with the weight of my sin as He hung on that cross. The difference was Jesus.

Bought and Paid For

I had come to God humble in my brokenness. As promised, I would go away justified. I could not move from my sin to a state of holiness any more than a slave can free himself. Try as I might, no amount of striving could make me a different person. No meditations on the beatitudes, hopes, and prayer for meekness, self-control, or compassion could take me beyond myself, my needs, my expectations of my husband, and my wants or see my husband differently. Not unlike a hamster on a wheel, running as hard as their small feet will allow, but completely stationary and not going anywhere. So mentally and emotionally fatigued that anything, even being divorced, robbing you, my daughter, of the childhood I envisioned for you, or even giving up in a different way, accepting a life of apathy and discontent, felt like a welcome rest over the daily battles. Have you not felt that sometimes? That you are running, juggling, trying, striving, as hard as you can, with as much energy as you can muster up, but all that it seems to produce is fatigue and exhaustion? Not just in marriage but in so many areas of our lives. I felt like that here, which is hard for a Type-A personality to admit, let alone accept. No, my daughter, that is not the life I wished for myself or the life I wish for you. And it is not the life that we need to live.

It's time to open that present, lying at the bottom of the Christmas tree, freely given but collecting dust, unopened, well past the due date of Christmas morning. Forgotten but no less valuable in what it contains; Grace.

"Come unto me, all ye that labor and are heavy laden, and I will give you rest. Take my yoke upon you, and learn of me; for I am meek and lowly in heart: and ye shall find rest unto your souls. For my yoke is easy, and my burden is light." - Matthew 11:28-30

We are fortunate to have a loving God who has asked us to *rest in Him* so that we do not need to bear the weight of trying to save ourselves, something we aren't even equipped to do! We can instead go to Jesus, lay down our sins and our shortcomings at his feet, and ask Him to remind us that He has already paid the price for that sin and that because of that ransom, we are *already free of it.*

In that darkest moment, I longed for a restoration of a relationship. I wanted happiness. But God was interested in something much deeper, at least at first. He was more interested in preparing me for eternity than in making me happy. That is not to say that joy was not around the corner. The Bible promises us, "Our mouths will be filled with laughter, our tongues with songs of joy" (Psalm 126:2). That is the hope we have as believers. But first, I had to allow myself to be molded by the potter in whatever way He sees fit.

Daughter, I know that is not something we ever want to hear, but I am writing this to you with so much love that my heart is about to burst. Suppose every circumstance and every challenge is an opportunity for us to grow in Christ-like character, one of our fundamental purposes of being on this earth. In that case, marriage will be one of the most significant challenges. After all, who goes into a marriage expecting, wanting, or thinking they will be the one who needs to change? I certainly did not. But is that doggedness or self-interest going to help me have a healthy, fruitful, joy-filled marriage that will last a lifetime? Possibly, probably, No.

If you aren't moving forward, I think you are not just stationary, you are slowly slipping backwards. I say this because I think life is sufficiently difficult so as to be an uphill battle where gravity constantly tries to pull you down. And as any couple who has been married for a long time would tell you, keeping a marriage thriving is even harder.

Daughter, though I have hope that it is possible, I cannot promise you that your marriage will be happy any more than I can guarantee that you will choose a good partner to marry. That is why it is important to make sure that you make a bed that you are willing to lie in for the rest of your life. But I do know that we are not alone in our struggles, that marriages are important to God, that He fights alongside us for our marriages, that He has given us the Holy Spirit as a helper, and that Jesus paid the price for our sinful behaviors so that we can be set free from our self-sabotaging thoughts and ways. Since I started writing this book, I have failed many times to live up to an embodiment of Jesus in my marriage and have consequently had many moments of repentance and frustration. But once in a while, I would be 'triggered' and find myself keeping my mouth shut or even being unaffected, and through the small wins, I am encouraged because it reminds me that we have been made into a new creation.

As for us, we were giggling and connected again with time, as you may have guessed from the start of these letters. True to my faith declaration, we expect our second child, a sister to our daughter, in a few months. Our adventure in a new continent has brought us closer together. Things are far from perfect, but I honestly could not ask for more. How could I, when I can hear the whispers of my husband's morning prayers floating into the bedroom before I am fully awake, and my heart is full of love, gratitude, and joy every time I think of him? Isn't that real perfection?

This feels like a good place to end my letter to you. Disappointed? I suppose you were hoping for stories of how we lived happily ever after.

When you look to understand the financial health of a Company, there are a few key documents that will be of interest; the profit and loss statement, the balance sheet, and the cash flow statement. Of these, the balance sheet is uniquely different in that it only shows you the state of the company *at a certain point in* time, as if you had taken a snapshot of it on a certain day. While it can reveal useful information about the company, it is unwise to use it as the only data point when assessing how well the company is doing, as it does not show the full picture. If you were to judge the company's health using only that snapshot in time, you would likely be led astray. I think marriage is a bit like that. There will be good days, great days, and difficult days in the entire lifespan of a marriage. I am encouraged by the small wins we have every day, the laughter, the companionship, the trust, the loyalty to keep going even in the trenches, and of course, our love and friendship. I hope we may live to a ripe old age, slow dancing and enjoying a glass of champagne in our sunset years, enjoying our children and grandchildren. But that might be a hard image to hold on to the next time there is a bad day. But remember, that day will be a snapshot in time and will not be a good basis to judge the entirety of marriage, and I hope that thought will encourage you the next time you feel like giving up.

And so, I embrace marriage for what it is—the joys and rewards. But mostly, one of the biggest opportunities I will have in this lifetime to be pruned, refined, and challenged in my journey as a follower of Christ. It isn't about my happiness (though I believe it will be a byproduct). It's about eternity.

And if things go well, I will one day hear the words I desperately long for:

"Well done, good and faithful servant."

mother

Nihara Guruge

6. a mother is forged

"The Lord had said to Abram, "Go from your country, your people and your father's household to the land I will show you. "I will make you into a great nation, and I will bless you; I will make your name great, and you will be a blessing.

I will bless those who bless you, and whoever curses you I will curse; and all peoples on earth, will be blessed through you" - Genesis 12:1-3

Daughter, if I were being honest with you, I have to admit that, left to my own devices, notions, and limited vision, you almost did not exist in this world.

You see, for the longest time, the identity that I had crafted for myself did not include the role of motherhood. I could see myself as a finance executive of a Fortune 500 company but could not imagine being pregnant or a mother. I had been very clear with my boyfriend/fiancé during marriage preparation that I did not find myself particularly enamored by the idea of small children, imagined I would be an awful mother at best, and did not relish the thought of childbirth, which frankly seemed traumatic on several levels. Besides, I had narrow hips and would surely die in childbirth based on my uneducated and limited understanding of the process at the time (I am much wiser now and can only think of these musings with intellectual embarrassment). Anyone who wanted to be my partner would need to be okay that it would just be the two of us and that *we* would be enough for a lifetime.

I still remember vividly one ordinary Sunday in Singapore after the church service ended that there was a call to go up to the altar to receive a blessing. My husband and I went up to the altar and joined the crowd, milling about the altar as the worship music played. It was customary for a few pastors to go through the crowd, whispering a prayer or blessing over the waiting crowd. Suddenly, I felt someone grab me from behind, a well-known pastor at our church whose sermons I had heard many times. She placed her hand on my womb from behind and started declaring that it was open and praying for children. Usually, we keep our eyes closed, and heads bowed for these prayers, but my eyes flew open to meet that of my fiancé, now husband, whose face was an unhelpful mixture of surprise and amusement, the latter probably more so at my reaction than anything. I felt indignant; I had not come up to ask for a baby.

Moreover, I wanted a blessing for my career, a desire that conflicted with the very prayer being declared over me now. Babies didn't help careers, at least not for women (though I would later find out motherhood did have its contribution to leadership, and babies didn't necessarily need to *hurt* careers either; more on that later). Needless to say, suddenly getting an unsolicited prayer for a baby shoved down my throat was less than welcome.

Still, we laughed about it over lunch, and I tried to put it out of my mind. I was disquieted, as no prayer or prophesy received at the altar had ever been wrong so far in my life, but perhaps there was a miscommunication with the radio frequency. I didn't suddenly have a desire for children and could not even fathom the idea of motherhood. I was just not wired that way. Best to put it out of my mind and move on.

Daughter, I joked about this during the introduction, but if God wants to tell you something, He will keep repeating the message louder and louder until you hear it. Over the next two years, God kept bringing me back to the covenant He made with Abraham and Sarah and His promise to extend their line through the birth of a son, long past the age they felt it was possible. I was hardly as old as Sarah, having just hit my early thirties, but I couldn't help but share in her disbelief, although it was for different reasons, such as my perceived unsuitability for the task. Much prayer and reflection later, I reluctantly accepted that *maybe* God was asking me to be open to motherhood, but I was still half hoping I was wrong. After a year or two of sitting on the idea, I became curious, even open, and wondered if I had been wrong or hasty all this time. I think I had to break the news to my husband over several conversations allowing him to digest this drastic change in my stance on the issue.

Nonetheless, I now felt that I was being imprisoned by my previously construed notions, bound by my false ideas of identity and fear, more than I was being true and open to this new calling. Just like not everyone is called into marriage, and some are called to be single, not everyone is called to motherhood, but I was using that as an excuse to justify *creating* my calling rather than listening to where God wanted to take me. About two years after that day at the altar, we started trying to expand our family. By the next month, January 2020, we would be blessed to see that positive test result.

The year started on a less than cheery note, with the 2019 Australian Bush fires continuing onto the new year that had devastating consequences to wildlife, destroying millions of acres of land, decimating thousands of homes, and killing hundreds of people. But on this side of the world, other than yet another news story shrugged off as similar to the Californian wildfires, which have their own dedicated spot in the news cycle, life continued. Goals were set for the year; plans were made, and everyone geared up for the new year. Shortly after that, we discovered that I was pregnant, and we were suddenly faced with the prospect of a year very different from the one we imagined ahead of us.

"Many are the plans in a person's heart, but it is the Lord's purpose that prevails" - Proverbs 19:21

The positive test result was, of course, met with joy, and then on my part, trepidation, mainly related to the upcoming birth and delivery experience, always portrayed as severely traumatic. I have had to experience a full journey to accept motherhood as a possibility for myself, and so the relative speed with which everything was happening felt to me like being on a runaway train. I know many women out there become pregnant and feel ready for the experience, but I was somewhat ready but mostly not. But something else lurking beneath that reared its ugly head; fear and anxiety, beasts that I did not even recognize at first, having rarely been encountered as the nemesis of my adventures. Pregnancy seems to start with that simple test and then get the ball rolling towards more tests, from blood draws, ultrasounds, and torturous glucose tests. At one of my early prenatal visits, the nurse helpfully said that I would master the skill of doing my business into a cup by the end of the pregnancy. Now there's a skill that can't make it to my resume. What a pity!

All this, of course, is to ensure that we have as much information as possible about the baby's growth in the womb, from the moment of conception to him or her opening their eyes in this world. Information is wonderful. Information can transform. Information can save. But information, like any other tool, needs to be used with wisdom, and I found myself in those early weeks falling into the pit of information related to pregnancy, parenting, health, diet, wellness, and all things related to anything and everything that can go wrong with this baby. Was I eating the right things to give optimal nutrition to the baby? Was I gaining sufficient weight? What if I ate something infected and had a miscarriage? What if I don't maintain a calm demeanor and my baby is born anxious and fretful, forever doomed to live a life full of stress due to my actions in these nine months? What if he or she doesn't get a good education? What if he or she is bullied, something I had never experienced in my childhood? *Was I making all the perfect decisions?*

And on and on, I kept spiraling.

In desperation to stop my anxious thoughts, I kept praying and reading the Bible. Daughter, this is how I know the Word is a living force; while I was reading a chronological bible reading plan in a very timely manner, I was studying how the Israelites wasted so much time wandering around in the desert, eventually building idols because they did not trust the God who brought them out of slavery. Perhaps I did not connect the dots on my own because one day, as I sat in the hallway, putting on my shoes, I suddenly heard as clear as day (in my heart, not a booming voice in the hallway lest you convict me to an asylum), *"Nihara, you have always thought that you were full of faith, but look at your unbelief! This is unbelief that you need to confess and repent, and commit to Me"*. It shocked me to hear this because I did not think faith in God was an area I needed to work on. I had seen Him do miraculous things in my life in the way of provision and did not think I doubted His sovereignty. And yet, I was spiraling with *worry* because of my unbelief.

"Peace I leave with you; my peace I give you. I do not give to you as the world gives. Do not let your hearts be troubled and do not be afraid.- John 14:27

In hindsight, this was just the start of God preparing me for the years ahead. If that was how I let worry consume me when all was good and well in the world, I can only imagine how I would have been consumed by it completely when you added on everything else yet to come our way in 2020. It took me weeks, but I asked for and received His peace. I took this baby, a mere embryo at the time, to God and committed his or her life to Him. I acknowledged that this life belonged to Him, not to my husband and me, that we will do everything within our power to love and raise this child to the best of our abilities for as long as we will have with them, but that ultimately it was God who was in control. We would later find out that we were expecting a girl, and when it came time to choose names, it was important for me to have my daughter's name reflect and honor this sentiment that she *belongs* to God, so we agreed on Liel.

With renewed faith, February rolled into March. I had heard rumblings of the pandemic through my friends and family in Asia, particularly in Singapore, with questions on whether this would be a repeat of the 2002-2004 SARS COV Outbreak in Asia, spreading to 29 countries before it was declared "contained" by the World Health Organization (WHO) in 2003 (with a few cases being seen as late as 2004). The first few cases were discovered in the new year, and the disease was identified and analyzed during the coming weeks of January and February. The genome was shared but had not made it to mainstream media. On January 30, 2020, the WHO declared the COVID-19 outbreak a global health emergency. On February 3rd, the USA declared a public health emergency. On March 11, 2020, the WHO declared COVID-19 a global pandemic. In March, I was on a business trip in Alabama and having breakfast with my colleagues when one of them, visiting from New York, shared that he had just heard that the state was going into lockdown in phases. While we had been hearing of cases for several weeks at that point, I felt the first inkling of concern when I heard him say that because my sister lived in New York.

We would eventually receive the work-from-home/stay-at-home order, and looking back, I believe that the majority of us believed that the two-week lockdown would be the peak of the pandemic. I was grateful, as I was battling severe first-trimester fatigue at the time, exacerbated by caffeine withdrawal, and thankful that I had a break from both business travel and the daily commute to the office. I could work from the comfort of my couch in peace, spending most of those two weeks with my legs up on a stool and taking one too many naps. I recognize how blessed I was to live such a luxurious life as there are millions of women out there every day, fighting the same fatigue while going to work or even hard labor. But most of all, I was grateful that when fear, worry, and anxiety started to rear its head again (*What if I got infected? What if my husband did? What if the baby is affected? What about my parents?*), I was not starting from scratch. The words in Psalms 91 that I had memorized as a young student attending a catholic school that we had parroted for years without fully realizing the full extent of them, words that I did not even remember were etched into my memory, started to float up to the surface.

"Whoever dwells in the shelter of the Most High will rest in the shadow of the Almighty.

I will say of the Lord, "He is my refuge and my fortress, my God, in whom I trust."

Surely He will save you from the fowler's snare and from the deadly pestilence.

He will cover you with his feathers, and under his wings you will find refuge; his faithfulness will be your shield and rampart.

You will not fear the terror of night, nor the arrow that flies by day,

nor the pestilence that stalks in the darkness, nor the plague that destroys at midday" – Psalm 91:1-6

Now, before you think reciting bible verses is part of the school curriculum in South Asia, let me give you some context.

I grew up in Sri Lanka, a small but extraordinarily beautiful island nation south of India. It had broken into the international limelight as many things in the past; the Lonely Planet destination of the year for its tourism, as the country with the world's first female prime minister in politics, the 1996

Cricket World Cup champions in sports, or even perhaps as the producers of some of the world's best tea. For historians, Sri Lanka is a country that boasts a history going back to prehistoric times, with thousands of years of kings, queens, and kingdoms painting a rich tapestry of history, today evidenced by the myriad of ancient temples and structures that attract tourists from all over the world.

It is certainly all that, but unfortunately, it has also seen more than its share of violence, with all-out conflict from 1983 ending only in 2009, which has resulted in casualties ranging from 60,000-100,000 in the decades of conflict between the government and the LTTE. According to the FBI, the Liberation of Tigers of Tamil Eelam (LTTE) was a militant group that perfected the use of suicide bombings, invented the suicide belt, and pioneered the use of women in suicide attacks in a war that ranged nearly three decades as one of the longest in Asia. The legacy of violence ended with war crimes and human rights violations against the primary victims of every war; civilians. While the combat was restricted to the North East of Sri Lanka, claiming the lives of many, Colombo saw its share of violence in the form of continuous suicide bombings, some of the deadliest in the history of the world. One particular deadly attack took place in 1996, vivid in my memory as the bomb went off while I was playing in the school yard with my friends during recess when we heard the loud explosion and felt and heard the windows of our school rattle. It is funny as while I do not remember much, I remember the exact location I was standing in the schoolyard. Parents were called to collect their children from school, but not all could make it in the middle of the day. Memories remain of seeing my mother go off to work at the World Trade Centre- another building continuously getting bomb threats. Our schools were not immune to bomb threats, and there were months we had to wear normal clothing instead of our usual school uniforms so as not to tip off the public that school was in session and attract an attack. We carried all our belongings in clear plastic school bags and pencil cases as opaque backpacks could be used to conceal explosives. We saw images on television of suicide bombings and presidents being assassinated. We heard of bus stations, public buildings, and other prominent landmarks being targeted. Every time there was an attack, we wondered if someone we knew had died. Checkpoints along the road that stopped and searched all vehicles were the norm, with some bombs still slipping through. One afternoon, I remember my mother, about to take me to the library to get me a membership as they couldn't keep up with my reading habits, hearing from my father that her brother in the Air Force, a pilot, had been flying an aircraft full of journalists had discovered too late that the insurgents now had surface to air missiles as we later found out from the Black Box remains. I was right next to her and my dad by the telephone as we received the call, and I vividly remember her breaking down crying, clutching the Rupee notes that were to be my subscription fee. I was nine but still older than my cousins, his two children.

Such was my childhood and that of many others in Sri Lanka, though many more children had it far worse in the war-torn areas. I thank God that I attended a Catholic school where at a young age, we as a school started to claim Psalms 91 during prayers every day without fail. We learned the words when we were young, but I would be reciting these words years later when we graduated. After the war ended, I did not think of those verses anymore, especially as I started work in Singapore, but as news of the pandemic spread, these verses, which were such a big part of my childhood, began to surface, brought up from the hidden recesses of my memory.

"Start children off on the way they should go, and even when they are old they will not turn from it" (Proverbs 22:6).

How true this is as ever so often the words would float back to my consciousness when I felt fear.

This time around, it wasn't a war against flesh but a war against an unseen virus. But the weapon was the same; fear.

I recommitted all that I could not control and my baby and my family to God. I placed a hand over my stomach and started to whisper these verses that seemed to be etched in my memory. Other parts of the Bible that I had been reading, sometimes even as a chore, started to float into my thoughts. How the people of Israel covered their doorframes with the lamb's blood so that the devourer would pass their homes without hurting their families. I imagined the blood of Jesus over my doorframe and visualized it every time I stepped through the threshold. I pondered how we are covered by the blood of an even more precious lamb, Jesus Himself, and how Satan could not cause havoc in Job's life or touch a hair on his head without God's consent.

"For He will command his angels concerning you to guard you in all your ways; they will lift you up in their hands, so that you will not strike your foot against a stone." – Psalms 91: 11-12

It was easy to be brave when it came to my own life; much harder to imagine harm coming to my loved ones, who I could no longer visit due to travel restrictions, and my sister who was in the epicenter of the disease at the time and so many other family members and friends. But as I pictured an imaginary stroke of blood over the doorframe of our new home, the thought that not a hair on our head can be touched without God's permission (which He may or may not grant in accordance with His purpose for me), finally gave me the kind of peace that I did not think was possible to have in this life. Now, I understand what Paul meant when he said in his letter to the Philippians, *"And the peace of God, which transcends all understanding, will guard your hearts and your minds in Christ Jesus" (Philippians 4:7)*. We are not on this earth to live perfect lives, experiencing no loss or sadness or regret, but we are on this earth to know God through all of life, in the valleys and the mountains, but for us believers who seek Him, who are under His protection, not a stone will hurt our heels without His consent. And if He consents, the word says that I can endure it. And endure it we will until we run our race and finally meet our just rewards in Heaven.

It was only March (in what I swear is the longest year in the history of mankind!), but the second personal battle of the year had been won. It might have been first-trimester fatigue, but that night I slept well.

And then came the nine minutes and thirty-second-long video that shook the world.

That is how long it took for the world to watch as George Floyd, a 46-year-old black man who went to a convenience store was killed. In May, the world watched in horror as the video of Mr. Floyd's murder was shared with anyone with a cell phone and an internet connection. People watched flabbergasted as the police officer continued to place his knee on Mr. Floyd's neck for two whole minutes after he was checked for a pulse and was found to have none, in broad daylight, surrounded by a crowd of witnesses. As bystanders circulated the video of his death, George Floyd became a rallying cry around the world, though perhaps nowhere as intensely as in the United States, against racism, institutional and otherwise, against police brutality and police accountability. Protests erupted across America, demanding everything from justice for Mr. Floyd to a massive revamping of unjust societal structures and institutions. The pandemic was forgotten for the next few weeks (though continuing to rage silently, killing thousands every week), and millions of protesters took to the streets to support the Black Lives Matter movement.

Michael Brown. Eric Garner. Tamir Rice. The list goes on. These names are known not just in America but around the world. I was no stranger to racism, having observed it in Sri Lanka and Singapore, but I had never experienced fear when encountering a police officer. The uniform filled me with a sense of safety and comfort. And the probability of a loved one coming to an untimely death was about the same as everyone else.

After I moved to Houston, people would often ask me what the most significant change was. How did I adjust? The answers were usually about the food (anyone who moved from Singapore to anywhere else on earth would say the same!), the public transportation or size of housing, or being able to drive a car! The honest answer, which I would never say out loud for fear of dousing the conversation with a shower of depression, was this: unlike in Singapore, in Houston, if my husband is late to come home or if I can't reach him on his mobile, I inevitably have the thought; *"has something happened to him because of the color of his skin?"*.

It was something I always squashed away without dealing with the underlying problem; fear. But when that video of George Floyd's murder started circulating, I couldn't even bring myself to watch it. It was all too close to home. Not only was my husband a Black man in America, but I would also soon be faced with the prospect of having to have a conversation with my daughter, who would at least partly identify as Black. I wouldn't just have to explain to her the dangers facing women in the world, but I would need to educate her that as long as she lived in America, she could not just break into our house if she forgot her key or that she can't stuff her hands in her pockets, even angrily, or that she can't act with the remotest amount of suspicion, even if she was a kid just playing on her block. That it wasn't fair, but she had to live by a different, stricter set of rules. Fear, dormant for a few weeks, roared again as I realized that, yet again, tired as I was, I would need to pick up my battered armor and limp into battle.

If the foundation of my faith was on even slightly more shaky ground, or if I hadn't been feeding it a constant stream of the Word of God for months, or years leading up to this point, I don't think I would have been able to be resilient at that moment, and I would not have been able to switch from survival mode to battle mode and win back the lost territory of my spirit. I was not fighting against flesh and blood but against spirits and principalities that are constantly trying to rob us of the joy and peace that has been freely given. I was immediately convicted of the truth; God is God, no matter where I live. If it was our time to go to Heaven and meet our Father, it would not matter whether I was living in the safest country in the world. Likewise, I could live in a country ravaged by war, safely and securely in the knowledge of His protection, that no hair on my head will be harmed while I was under His protection unless He wills it so.

"I have told you these things, so that in me you may have peace. In this world you will have trouble. But take heart! I have overcome the world." – John 16:33

The battle against anxiety is not one and done. It sometimes feels as though women tend to worry more than men. I don't see this as condemnation. However, I think even Jesus knew He would need to speak to some of us in this area, as we saw when He visited the house of Martha and Mary and said in Luke 10: 41-42, *"Martha, Martha, thou art careful and troubled about many things: But one thing is needful: and Mary hath chosen that good part, which shall not be taken away from her."* I love that the example to follow that He highlighted here was also another woman, which is so encouraging to see! We are not called to be like men but instead, the best version of ourselves we can be as women. Armed with this, I know that the battle against worry, fear, and anxiety would be one that I have to watch out for all my days, that it won't be won in one battle or even five or five hundred. Every day I live, there will be forces trying to rob me of my joy. There are a million reasons not to have peace in your mind; all you need to do is look around you in the world.

But there is one very good reason that you *should* have peace: Jesus.

7. a mother is born

"Consequently, just as one trespass resulted in condemnation for all people, so also one righteous act resulted in justification and life for all people." – Romans 5:18

A pregnant woman stands with her friends, talking. Suddenly, there is a gush of water, and she exclaims that her water has broken! She is rushed to the hospital and starts pushing. Her face contorts with unbearable pain as she experiences the worst pain of her life, and she is angry at her husband. Moments later, a child is born. The pain is forgotten, and she goes home with her baby and slips into motherhood, marred only by the constant crying of an inconsolable baby. Unfortunately, this common scene in many Hollywood television shows or movies was my only preconceived notion about my impending childbirth experience. The worst pain imaginable, with my only respite being pain relief offered by medication that I would be yelling at the doctor to administer in between my screams of pain. It was a dreaded event, making me despise my womanhood and the unfairness of the cross I have to bear that my husband did not. A special punishment meted out to the woman in a life full of harsh judgment. It was a vivid enough picture to make me stay well away from motherhood for a good portion of my adult life.

When I eventually became pregnant, I was confronted with all my worst fears, previously buried deep within, or worse, on full display at the surface, totally normalized in the world as a part of the process that women must accept and tolerate. The birthing process was just something we had to get over, and hopefully, with minimal trauma and scars left behind. With that intent, I dove headfirst into the mind-numbingly horrifying world of episiotomies and pain medication. I looked for every possible way I could prepare my body physically for the upcoming trauma in nine months. I could not help but be resentful towards Eve for taking that bite of the apple or for Adam's passive relinquishment of headship that led to the punishment we are all familiar with; "I will make your pains in childbearing very severe; with painful labor, you will give birth to children" (Genesis 3:16). This is usually where the story ends with an expectation of pain and suffering being synonymous with childbirth. I took it for granted, with nothing and no one in life saying otherwise.

While diving into this unwanted world of pain and fear, I was also seeking God, though it was to seek relief from my anxiousness and worries about the future of this child and less about the actual labor and delivery experience. Because of the pandemic restrictions, my regular afternoon walk became the highlight of my day, often becoming my daily meditation, prayer and worship walk, the only time I was truly alone. It was on one such walk, some time in my first trimester, as I walked along the Buffalo Bayou with the mid-afternoon sun warming my bones, I was thinking about hospitals and birthing classes when suddenly I felt in my spirit, "something is not quite right." I stopped abruptly, unsure of what to make of this unbidden thought.

It would be a thought that would return to me over a few days before I opened up the Bible and read the familiar verses in Genesis 3:16, but instead of stopping there, I flipped over to the New Testament, forty-two books later, to another familiar passage, this time John 3:16, "For God so loved the world that He gave His one and only Son, that whoever believes in Him shall not perish but have eternal life." This was what did not feel right. A God who so loved us and gave us His son for our salvation does not sound like a God who is handing out curses and punishments today. I kept reading and eventually reached Romans 5:18, "Consequently, just as one trespass resulted in condemnation for all people, so also one righteous act resulted in justification and life for all people," and I took a deep breath. This was the missing piece. Here was the evidence that the price of sin was paid, the punishment was borne, and the curse was broken. We are no longer under the same judgment, so we can't possibly be under the same punishment! Yes, there was a fall due to original sin, but there was also redemption as the price was paid. This was what felt wrong; I was still living through the lens of punishment, but the reality, the truth, was that I was planted in freedom.

There is a beautiful painting called 'Virgin Mary consoles Eve' by Sister Grace Remington, a copy of which hangs in my home. There is an accompanying poem that goes:

"My mother, my daughter, life-giving Eve, Do not be ashamed, do not grieve. The former things have passed away, Our God has brought us to a New Day. See, I am with Child, Through whom all will be reconciled. O Eve! My sister, my friend, We will rejoice together Forever Life without end."

There is now a small growing movement among Christian doulas and even women outside the Christian community, attempting to educate and empower women regarding their labor and delivery experience. There are two broad aspects to this preparation. One is the physical (Yoga, Lamaze, understanding of our bodies through science), and the second is the mental and spiritual aspects. I confess, except for one five-hour birth preparation class that I took with my husband (who, to his misfortune, only asked me how long the class was when we were well on the way to the location; "Ha, for a moment, there I thought you said five hours!"), my physical preparation only consisted of daily walks. Instead, my mental and spiritual battle consumed my energy from the beginning.

Two thoughts begged my attention. First and foremost, the *pain* or *labor* with which children were to be born.

Some of my less than fond childhood memories are of my squash crew meeting up day in and day out before sunrise every morning for fitness training, often requiring us to wake up a bit after 5 am, chug a couple of barely cooked eggs, and a banana and make our way to the training grounds in haste. My sister and I played squash at the national level, and much of our childhood, when not in school, was spent either on the field or inside the court. I remember starting each session with a light warm-up of doing 15 or so rounds around the cricket field before starting on the high-intensity repetitions and ending the sessions with some pushups or sit-ups during the cooldown, all before 7 am when the sun starts to beat down a bit too hard for outdoor workouts to be comfortable. Besides, we often had to shower quickly and head to school, so workouts usually ended by sunrise. Since we did not have to rush to school during summer vacation, we enjoyed in-court training after the grueling outdoor training session, making the practice time last 4-5 hours. Naturally, it was not uncommon to experience *pain* which was usually muscle aches or a stitch on the side. Nothing acute of course, as that would signify an injury, rather, almost a pleasurable sort of strain on the muscles followed by an endorphin rush. The absence of this was usually an indicator that we were not pushing ourselves to the limit. And why did we push ourselves so hard? Because we knew that anything worth having usually required commitment and not an insignificant amount of effort, or dare I say, *labor*. The last thing you wanted was for your opponent to be enduring worse pain than you in the training field, only to be able to outlast you inside the court during game time.

This is where I urge you to find your own revelation about what the scripture decrees through prayer, meditation, and research. I wondered if the pain portrayed here was yet another form of *labor*, which would not be an unreasonable precursor for something as wondrous as bringing a new life into the world. Following this thought with the punishment being lifted through the death of Christ, I felt that we were taken back to the original vision for childbirth, a labor of love, not done alone or endured as punishment, but in partnership with the God who Himself 'pulls the babe out of the womb' (Psalm 71:7). I would even go further to note that there are many testimonies out there of women who give birth to children completely pain-free and Christian doulas who, through the support of scripture and encouragement, can guide you in this journey of realization. Certainly, countless women would testify that the labor itself, while difficult, is bearable, something that I would discover for myself with my second birth experience. Do not just accept what is presented to you by the world as truth; seek out the truth in the word of God.

Daughter, do not then underestimate the work that is required for labor. Science shows that childbirth can be as hard on the body as running a marathon and can even result in similar injuries. Anecdotal evidence suggests that it is even harder. Approach this with the attitude of an athlete approaching the biggest game or sporting event of their life with careful preparation and disciplined effort. But do not, under any circumstances, approach it with fear, for 'God does not give us a spirit of fear, but of power, love and sound mind.' Fear of childbirth was the single most effective tool created by the enemy to rob me of what would be the most meaningful event of my life. Armed with this, I started to approach my labor and delivery with nervous anticipation as I would be before an important exam or match, but with a sense of curiosity and expectation, wondering what God could and would do.

There is another truth to consider, and that is that our bodies are extraordinarily equipped for this process. I have always loved science. I find the more we discover about the world or ourselves through science, the more I am in awe of creation. Nothing brings this to light more than what goes through the female body during pregnancy. First-trimester lethargy and fatigue are often highlighted, but not much is said about why. A week after conception, energy is expended in our bodies as it starts to grow a whole new organ from scratch, the placenta. Once formed, the placenta and umbilical cord allow you to provide nutrients to your baby. It removes the baby's intrauterine waste and can even excrete hormones like human chorionic gonadotropin, estrogen, and progesterone. Those hormones maintain the pregnancy and prepare the mammary glands for nursing. Wonder how an eight-pound baby can come out of you? Throughout pregnancy, your body starts to release a hormone called relaxin that relaxes the ligaments in the pelvis and softens and widens the cervix.

The baby does not come out of you tearing and destroying. Instead, your body starts to shift its skeletal bone structure to accommodate the delivery and then, a while later, goes back to what it used to be! Your blood volume increases by at least 50% and your breathing capacity by 30-40%, supporting this new host environment. I once tried a sip of red wine in the second trimester as someone I was with was drinking what was said to be an exceptionally good variety. I found it repugnant, my taste buds instantly rejecting it on behalf of my body. I craved eggs, salads with broccoli, fruits, and oats (unfortunately, also a pint of chocolate ice cream per day which somehow was not rejected by my taste buds). My husband continued to stock up on the usual grocery list post-delivery, including my favorite chocolate ice cream, and weeks later realized that since delivery, I had not touched any of the things I used to eat daily throughout the nine months.

Daughter, believe in that purpose. You can do this. Your body can do this.

"But now, this is what the Lord says—he who created you, Jacob, he who formed you, Israel: "Do not fear, for I have redeemed you; I have summoned you by name; you are mine. When you pass through the waters, I will be with you; and when you pass through the rivers, they will not sweep over you.

When you walk through the fire, you will not be burned; the flames will not set you ablaze." – Isaiah 43:1-2

I will leave you with one final truth that I have discovered; we are not passive participants or observers in the birthing process any more than we are left sorely alone to bear the full brunt of the labor. Instead, childbirth is a unique opportunity (like building a church or raising an army for God) to partner with God to bring forth life, but one uniquely reserved for us women.

The miracle doesn't end with pregnancy, and God does not check out right before delivery. While I had an easy pregnancy and no complications, my doctor strongly urged me to induce labor as I slipped past thirty-nine weeks. I was devastated as this was absolutely not in my extensive birth plan. I held out for as long as possible, trying long walks and induction massages, hoping and praying to go into labor naturally. I kept praying to God to give me the birth I wanted, according to the schedule I wanted, but reluctantly ended every prayer with, 'your will be done' and thanking God for the promise that whatever the outcome, it would be 'Good' and according to His purpose. My mother and godmother urged me not to try too hard, that it would happen when it was meant to be. When my due date came and went, reluctantly, we checked into the hospital and started the induction.

The induction (or perhaps local hospital policies) meant I was strapped to the bed with limited movement. This greatly hampered my ability to use movement to reduce the impact of the contractions. My poor husband massaged my back for almost fourteen hours as I was induced using the Cook Catheter, an induction tool well known for greatly multiplying pain in the mother. Due to the pandemic, no doulas were allowed, so when my husband needed a break, I was on my own, trying to breathe through the contractions while not even being able to sit on a birthing ball. My only respite was the playlist of worship music that I had prepared beforehand, and I prayed that even when I was too tired to notice it, something was going through my spirit to reach my spirit and my daughter. When I could, I kept asking my husband to read out the scripture verses I had prepared beforehand, even when I did not have the energy to remind myself of God's promises to me. I hung onto the verse, "when you pass through the waters, I will be with you; and when you pass through the rivers, they will not sweep over you," as if my life depended on it.

After 14 hours of contractions coming in every 2-5 mins due to the induction, I thought I was ready to push but was told instead that I was ready to get started on the Pitocin, known to make contractions much worse. At this point, I had not had any food or water for almost eighteen hours and had no sleep for over a day. I was so exhausted that I finally decided to take an epidural despite my deep desire for a natural medication-free birth. I was further disappointed because I mistakenly thought that being as natural as possible in the process was the only way to experience God in the birthing process. But this was going to be my best chance of making sure I still had the energy to push when the time came. I had many expectations and plans for my birth (and an extensive birth plan). From the moment of induction, it felt like I might be getting further and further away from the amazingly natural spiritual birth I had seen in documentaries, where women seem to 'pop' them out in the car park and keep walking into the hospital. I worried that the birth would not be the spiritually fulfilling event I was hoping it would be. Would a different doctor, hospital, or any other number of choices have made a difference? I was asking, 'did I mess up my part in this, potentially ruining God's ability to deliver on His promise?' My faith was colliding with my need to be in control of outcomes, outcomes that I had no control over in the first place, and I needed to 'let go and let God.' All I had to do was believe God could still answer my prayer.

Finally, it was time to push. The adrenalin surge that set in when I started had me shivering and shaking (which I thought was due to the cold until the kind nurses pointed out that it was not). I heard my OBGYN exclaim, "are you sure you haven't done this before"? I wish I had the energy to give her a witty, sarcastic reply, but my lips felt dry, and I was in no mood to talk. Now I know that she had meant the speed with which my daughter was coming, given that I was a first-time mother or the ease with which my body was accommodating her birth (which only later after birth would I realize how fortunate I was). It seems my daughter, who did not want to come out at forty weeks, no longer wanted to hang around after the contractions started and was now in a hurry to come out. After only 30-40 minutes of pushing, there she was, lying on my chest, looking at me with wide-open eyes and a half smile on her face. The euphoric high that I experienced at that moment was a gift. The first photograph I have of her is her gazing at me with a half-smile on her face (as if to remind me that she did, indeed, do most of the work descending the birth canal herself!). I'm not sure what it is like for women who go through this without medication, but I could not imagine it being any better. While we had been whispering prayers throughout the night with worship music playing in the background, God was certainly there with me in that singular moment. He had answered my prayer. My daughter was good. Even though I couldn't have my mother or a doula there as planned due to COVID-19 restrictions, the experience was precious between my husband and me. In the end, that, too, was good. Nothing had gone according to my plan, but here I was on the other side, with a relatively unscathed body and a beautiful, healthy baby girl. I had done my part, my husband his, and God did His part, which with the benefit of hindsight, I realize was the heavy lifting. My prayer for a good birth was answered, and I had nothing but thankfulness and joy in my heart.

Daughter, I am tempted to end my letter here, but what came next, the post-partum period or the fourth trimester, as they say, was so hard, and much harder than the birth itself, that I would be negligent in my duty were I to omit to mention it altogether.

Physically, the recovery was a blast. No tearing, cutting, or surgery meant that I was pretty much able to get on with life pretty quickly. But I was in for a terrible surprise that I felt no one had warned me about. Throughout pregnancy, I would say that I couldn't wait until my body felt like it was my own again, freeing my choices and giving me back the full mobility and freedom that I was used to. If anything, the reality of what followed was far from that expectation.

I had not even taken a breastfeeding class, being told many times that it was the most natural thing in the world; perhaps that is the case if you happen to have your mother next to you helping, but my husband and I were very much alone in this due to the quarantine. I failed and gave up early when we needed to add formula into the mix due to the onset of jaundice, but I valiantly kept trying to nurse/pump for almost two months afterward with very little success. With a bit more education, I am now much more cognizant of all the things I could have done differently, but at the time, with no encouragement or support structure around me, all I felt was failure and isolation. Perhaps everything was exacerbated by the fact that between feeding, burping, rocking the baby, and pumping in my free time, I felt less than human, let alone a woman. One of my dear friends, who had children much earlier than me, once told me over dinner that she felt 'like a cow' once the baby was born, unable to even leave the house (when she, too, did not have a support structure being immigrants in their country). I don't think I understood the gravity of what she was sharing at the time, but time and experience have given me a little bit more perspective and appreciation now.

Even as I struggled with a low milk supply, I was shocked at how often I heard the question, "well, when do you plan to have the next one," when I was still bleeding from the baby I just had. The question, I felt, reduced me to nothing more than cattle. The next most frequent question was whether I would now quit my job and stay at home full time. All in all, perhaps I expected to hear this in Asia but not in the USA, which makes me wonder what it must be like for women who give birth in even more socially conservative countries. I held onto my poker face and gave flippant answers, but inside, I felt like I was being swallowed up by quicksand, triggering an identity crisis that I would talk about more in my letter, "Breaking all the rules." I had my husband with me, but in a way, he was not with me as I was alone in this. He could not understand why nursing was important to me. He was not being challenged to his very core about possibly giving up all that he enjoyed in life, which stimulated him in exchange for, yes, the greatest blessing of my life, my daughter, but it was still no easy thing to accept. He was not worried about his career trajectory or if his life was now permanently on a different course altogether.

Due to the pandemic, this was the first time I was not physically attending church and benefiting from corporate worship or seeing our church family regularly. It would be many months before we would do so out of an abundance of caution. It was the period in my life that I most needed worship and time along with God's word, but like hitting the snooze button on the alarm, I would forego being plugged into the source completely, sleep deprived, exhausted, and overwhelmed. My only respite was the lullaby I would sing to my daughter, for its easy, repetitive lyrics, 'Holy Spirit, you are welcome in this place,' which always seemed to fill my cup just a little bit with the bonus of calming my daughter. It was one of the loneliest times in my life, and I feel, in some way, it set the stage for all the stresses in our relationship that followed. In hindsight, I cannot help but question what price I paid in self-isolation in exchange for a manufactured sense of security from the virus.

Daughter, if nothing else, remember this. Walking through life alone is a choice, but it was not the path God intended for us. An army of women have felt every ache and pain, shed every tear, and felt every midnight moment of frustration when the baby would not stop crying. There is a church sitting behind you, ready to welcome you and help you. Above all, learn from my mistake; whatever you do, do not cut off the very source of life that sustains us; without God, we cannot do anything.

"Rejoice always, pray continually, give thanks in all circumstances; for this is God's will for you in Christ Jesus." -1 Thessalonians 5:16-18

I will leave you with one final word of encouragement; be it before conception, during pregnancy, childbirth, or post-partum, one thing that only got me through; prayer. I used to pray over my belly daily, even a few times a day. It was an easy way of relieving my anxiety and fears, as

I had already shared, but it was also more than that. Prayer, specifically bold prayers that asked for too much, that tested the limits of my imagination, have unlocked blessings in my life that I did not even think were possible. A baby that came out smiling who cried only when she needed food, a good burp, or gas, who has been sleeping twelve hours a night from when she was four months old; A child who breaks out into laughter so easily that she is joy personified. I've witnessed a prayer for protection being answered as I saw a toddler fall backward onto a flight of cement steps and get up unscathed, not even a pebble in her hair. I've seen a prayer for healing, one made in agreement between two people, move an arm that was otherwise lying limp. Most of all, a baby, a daughter, a child who has truly felt like a blessing to be enjoyed, bringing so much laughter and joy into the home.

So, pray boldly, my daughter, and pray for the impossible. You might just be paying God a compliment.

Nihara Guruge

worker

Nihara Guruge

8. tapestry

The Weaver – By Grant Colfax Tullar

My life is but a weaving
Between my God and me.
I cannot choose the colors
He weaveth steadily.
Oft' times He weaveth sorrow;
And I in foolish pride
Forget He sees the upper
And I the underside.
Not 'til the loom is silent
And the shuttles cease to fly
Will God unroll the canvas
And reveal the reason why.
The dark threads are as needful
In the weaver's skillful hand
As the threads of gold and silver
In the pattern He has planned
He knows, He loves, He cares;
Nothing this truth can dim.
He gives the very best to those
Who leave the choice to Him.

Two weeks before Christmas of 2020, our first Christmas as parents (thanks to our two-month-old bundle of joy, snot, and throw-up), my phone rang. I was still away from work on maternity leave, but I answered as I was expecting this particular call from my supervisor. I knew the call would be about whether my job was affected by the recent restructuring effort and if I would be at risk of being laid off.

Up to this point, I had been on a blessed path as far as my career was concerned, going from what felt like one dream job to another. Even a door that felt ambitious at the time, the Corporate NBD team, opened one day out of the blue. I still remember exactly where I was when I received that acceptance call. My husband and I were on holiday in Taiwan at the time with a mutual friend, and at that exact moment, I got the 'BBM' (only those Gen X-ers or Millennials who had owned a blackberry at the time would get this reference; for the rest, it means 'message'), I was about to board a carriage to zipline across Taipei. My husband took a photo of my face as I read the message, which accurately reflects the expression of one who had punched above their weight and now had to drink a heady cocktail of excitement mixed with a shot of fear, a dash of trepidation, shaken not stirred. It would be the start of one of the most exciting periods of my career, spanning eight years of deals in multiple continents and numerous business areas with ever-increasing size and complexity. My company was doing some big things, and I was on the front lines. I was growing, stretching, learning, energized, and confident that I was exactly where God wanted me to be, such was the harmony between my aspirations and talents.

All this to say, I was one of the fortunate few who could always say that I had always had the opportunities to take on roles that had energized me, and perhaps extra-fortunately, roles that I was half decent at. The move to Houston was easy, seamless, and hardly a challenge, as I kept doing more of what I enjoyed doing anyway, knowing I had a couple of years ahead of me before I started to get restless.

Therein lay the problem. As I would come to realize, 'easy' is a good breeding ground for restlessness. I wouldn't say the nature of what I was doing was easy per se, but I had always gone from one achievement to another, from as far back as when I was in my teens, and suddenly, like an addict, I wasn't getting the same hit with the same dosage. I wanted more. Less than ideal perhaps that the restlessness started to set in around 2019, which, unknown to us at the time, would herald through a few of the most difficult years for most on the planet. But in blissful ignorance, I started praying to God and asking for the next cool thing, the next open door, the next promotion. The only reality I knew was that if I wasn't moving forward and progressing, I was stagnating.

If I look back on my life, I can't pinpoint exactly when I became this way, measuring progress in life through achievements, going from one thing to the other, seeking affirmation in both trophies and accomplishments. A counselor once asked me, "when you were a child, how did your parents praise you?". I thought hard and answered with a laugh, "Can you explain the question, please? You see, we are Asian". Certainly, as some children with Asian parents would tell you, praise is something to be earned based on what we *do,* not who we are. I wouldn't exchange my parents or childhood for anything. I think I hit a remarkable jackpot in terms of both my parents and the childhood I was blessed to enjoy, and if I could give my daughters a semblance of that childhood, I have full confidence that they would turn out as at least, half decent human beings. But one thing we often lacked were words of encouragement. They were few and far between, extracted with the same ease as one would pull teeth out of a very angry tiger. But a trophy never failed to extract praise.

Indeed, culture cannot be ignored any more than its effect on us can be overlooked. Culture and perhaps the insecurities of my youth, where I felt the need to set myself apart and be seen, valued, and appreciated. Or perhaps, it was none of these things. I'd been to enough personality profiling courses to think maybe I was just wired this way, competitive, ambitious, and always wanting more. But accomplishments are not the enemy. After all, we are on earth to be productive and fruitful. Each of us is given unique talents and gifts, and as Jesus explained, our reward will be measured based on how we use those gifts in the limited time we have on this earth.

The problem, though, was that without my conscious awareness, I was, for decades, relying on and pursuing achievements, promotions, and the praise of others to affirm, to feel worthy, or to feel valued.

Isn't that just human?

Sure.

But does that make it right?

No, I don't think so.

Is that what God wants for us?

Definitely not.

I once had a supervisor to whom I reported for a few months and, arguably, had very little interaction with saying this of me; "solid performer, not remarkable."

Not remarkable.

His casual remark about me upset me so much that I was upset for days. Even as I write this today, years later, I can still feel the exact sting I felt when I heard those words. I felt lower upon hearing those words than I ever felt high when I received an equal or greater praise report along the lines of 'I believe in you, and that you can do anything you set your mind to doing'. Over years of positive, encouraging feedback did not have the same impact as that casual negative remark. Daughter, I urge you to be careful with your words. Once they leave your lips, you can never take them back.

For years, I had let these highs and lows, at the hands of jobs, deals, colleagues, bosses, and even loved ones, run unchecked, affecting my moods and emotions. After all, measuring our worth or potential and comparing that worth against the person sitting next to us is an institutionalized practice in most companies. The 'norm' as far as the Human Resource strategy for talent management goes.

And there I was, praying, hoping, searching, and networking my way through to the next big thing, when March 2020 hit the world.

To many, the pandemic of 2020-2022 was an opportunity to reset and refocus on what was important, and we were no different. Only when you were not allowed to leave your home will you become starkly aware of how busy and crammed our lives are. Between work, church commitments, social activities, and family obligations, my husband and I hardly seemed to spend any time alone anymore, so much so that the forced shutdown in March of 2020 seemed almost like an answered prayer. Looking back, I would often share that the quality time we got alone together, just the two of us, was a much-needed boost ahead of our family expanding to include a permanent plus one. That the first shutdown at a global level coincided with my first-trimester nausea and fatigue, allowing me a solid two weeks of rest on the couch, was a blessing to me. Despite the chaos and trauma around us, the year will forever be marked in my conscious as one of the best of my life as it brought forth my daughter into our lives, forever changing the course and nature of the steps we would take from now on.

The next year was a different beast altogether.

The dawn of a new year is typically hailed with celebration and thanksgiving while we bid a fond farewell to the departing year. It was therefore somewhat surprising to wake up to the following headline in Colombo shortly before New Year's Eve 2022: "Good riddance to the doom and gloom of 2021". I couldn't help but smile in agreement. 2020 was difficult, but not in my personal opinion, as difficult as 2021. I would later reflect on the year and think I was being put through spiritual bootcamp. In hindsight, I would later realize it was a year of tearing down to build up anew. To strengthen the foundation, reveal and remove weaknesses, and weather-proof the structure ahead of the things to come.

The dead halt in global transportation from 2020 onwards and, to an extent, consumption in some sectors led to an inevitable industry-wide restructuring effort in the energy sector (where I worked) that was hitherto unseen in my career to date. What need did we have for gas if we had nowhere to drive our cars? No offices to commute to, restaurants to frequent, or children's school activities to fit into our schedules? What use of airplanes when countries around the world started shutting down borders? Some sectors were booming, of course; production of Iso-Propyl alcohol (hand sanitizer) was through the roof, and so was any ancillary petrochemical business associated with global healthcare, masks, and other preventive measures. For some hitherto unexplained reason, so was the sale of toilet paper rolls.

After months of planning, the much-anticipated new organizational structure, expected to make our company more resilient and competitive in this new challenging environment, was unveiled. I was expecting the call when my phone rang. I answered, more eager for some clarity than anything else. The uncertainty of not knowing has been infinitely worse than dealing with bad news. I sat on the stairs and listened.

All employees at my level were supposed to be out of scope and 'safe.' But due to a glitch in the HR system, I was not. I alone, among all my peers, would be at risk and need to apply for my role in a few months. If I wanted to do something different, I would need to compete for a promotion with the entire population of people with more experience than me. It would be a minimum of six to nine months before the full process is completed.

Not the best news to receive just before the holidays, but at least now I know what I am praying for. Better to deal with the mountain before you than not knowing at all.

My mind raced through the initial reactions to the news.

A system glitch? That is by far one of the stupidest things I have ever heard.

I'm relatively new to the country; do I have enough of a track record to secure my job? Do I have enough people in my network?

Will I be made redundant? Will I have to look for a job in another company during a global recession?

Why is this happening?

Is this you, God? A system glitch that singles me out? Are you going to perform some big miracle and get me some amazing job again?

Okay, that is probably it. Otherwise, this is just too random. We don't go through things for the sake of going through them. God is probably about to open a new door, just like I had been praying for.

I did not want to share this particular chapter. It did not feel good. But I want to make sure I never forget that feeling of receiving that call because I might have to make that call one day. Or my daughter or husband, or friend or family member might get that call, and it is the kind of call that unless you have been on the receiving end of it, followed by months of uncertainty, you can never really understand the emotional scar it leaves behind, even if you emerge relatively unscathed.

Once the initial shock wore off, I looked for how I could process this information in a way that fitted with my worldview. Perhaps, this was not just a terrible thing to happen to me. Perhaps, such a bewildering and random event, such as being at risk of severance because of a technical system error, was surely happening so that God can open a new door for me, one I had been hoping for. Maybe this terrible thing was happening so He could provide me with something better.

Amidst this drama, our house suffered some damage during the winter storm in Texas (yes, I said winter), and through a series of delays, poor project management on the part of the contractor, and our decision to get the house into an even better condition than when we bought it, what started as a two-week job instead stretched out for months caused by supply chain delays in the industry. But even with a house renovation going on while working on two high-speed deals, I didn't spend a day without thinking about my job. I would wake up thinking about it and go to sleep worried about it. Peace was the furthest thing from my heart. It was a bitter and despondent feeling for someone who has never struggled with closed doors. I redoubled my efforts in figuring out my next move; perhaps God was ending a season in my life with a Company that I loved. A door seemed to open with a competitor, more pay for the same work; perhaps that is the door? But I couldn't quite find peace with that decision. Until this point, the next step had always been so apparent and obvious, like an illuminated door in a dark room, and for the first time, I felt lost in the dark, unsure of what was next.

Throughout the year, I experienced many highs and lows, mainly as I made my plans and backup plans to my plans and tried to work out all the angles I could think of to try to fix this on my own, to try to orchestrate the impossible. I dealt with crushing blows to my confidence at not getting any of the jobs I had applied for. The devastation and insecurity that seeps in when you think, perhaps, I am not what I thought I was, maybe I was not as good as I thought. Perhaps, I will never be what I hope to be, and maybe my ambitions exceed my capabilities. I kept asking God, "why are you allowing me to go through this? Why is this necessary?" The only thing I didn't do, which would have saved me a lot of grief and time, was to take a moment to pause, pray and listen to what God was telling me to do. Had I done so, I could have spent more time working on myself and my spiritual growth than on my CV.

As time dragged on, I swiftly moved on from denial, anger, and rationalization into the next and might as say, the least enjoyable stage of grief; depression. Not in the clinical sense, but I started to lose my hair, always seemed to live a hair length away from irritability, and struggled with insomnia for the first time in my life. The last one was a wake-up call, as getting that solid seven to eight hours of sleep every night has always been my superpower. I started to look forward to that glass of wine at the end of the day a bit too much. Mostly I feared that I was being called to leave behind full-time work in a company I loved or being asked to tamper down my dreams and ambitions. But surely, if God didn't want me to have a career in this way, *why* did He make me like this? Constantly needing intellectual stimulation, driven, ambitious, always wanting to do big things?

Charles Spurgeon once said, *"You are as much serving God in training your own children as you would be if you lead an army to battle for the Lord."* I've been blessed to experience both staying at home, be it due to maternity leave or a period of transition, and being fully engaged at work. I found being a full-time mother to a baby/toddler a hundred times more difficult. Compared to constantly being on your feet, with limited social interactions, continually going from one task to the next, I would gladly welcome being buried in an excel spreadsheet, music playing over my headphones while sitting at my office chair for ten to twelve hours a day. But difficulty aside, between the two roles, I know which one had me getting out of bed energetic and excited and which role had me dragging myself out of bed in the morning, counting down the minutes and hours until my 'shift' was over. I applaud with enormous respect the men and women who derive great fulfillment from staying at home, but unfortunately, I know I am just not wired in that way, at least not at this point in my life (I've learned never to say never).

At no point did I think, perhaps, God was showing me that there was an idol in my life that I hadn't even realized was an idol. Perhaps for my whole life, a large portion of my identity was tied to my accomplishments, career, and ambitions. I had always perfectly reconciled my goals and aspirations for my career with my Christian faith, wholly sure that God supported my 5, 10, 15-year career plan. Now, I was forced to consider; had I asked God what I should do, or had I asked Him to bless my plan? Did I know who I was anymore if I didn't have any accomplishments to my name? Yes, of course, I was a wife, mother, daughter and sister, friend and ally, and follower of Jesus.

But did any of those roles make up as much a part of my identity as my career?

I once heard *an idol* defined in the following way by my pastor in Houston; "An idol is anything you rely on for some blessing, help or

guidance in the place of a wholehearted reliance on the true and living God."
I was fairly confident that I did not worship my job. Nor do I think if asked
directly to choose between a career and God, I would have picked anything
other than my God. But then why should I be so fearful and devastated at the
thought of this *thing* being taken away from me? Finally, after months of
constantly asking and talking, I decided to shut up and listen. And there in
the quiet stillness was the whisper of an answer that seemed so loud that
surely it was echoing through the streets; *"I am trying to set you free, my
child."*

"Free from what!" I nearly screamed in frustration. "I didn't worship my
career"!

*"Perhaps not, but you have allowed it to define you. You have come to
rely on it for your identity and joy and upon the accomplishments of your
hands for your sense of well-being and self-worth. And I want you to define
yourself only in Me and through Me".*

Faced with that unwanted mirror being held up, I was forced to confront
two hard truths.

One, I have placed an over-reliance on my career and accomplishments
to define my identity and make me feel good, worthy, and deserving of praise
and appreciation. My identity and self-worth, instead, needed to be firmly
based on who God says I am. Not a trophy or a job, a performance review,
or the praise of a colleague, a promotion or lack thereof, or even defined by
my past. Instead of acting like a daughter of God who happens to be engaged
in productive work, I am looking to earn my position and status in life
through the work of my hands.

God says that I have been fearfully and wonderfully made; that His works
are wonderful (Psalm 139:13-14). Therefore, it stands to reason that my very
existence must be miraculous. That the very hair on my head, even the ones
that seem to be jumping ship like rats, is numbered by Him (Matthew 10:30).
And most amazingly, that I am created in the very image of God (Genesis
1:27). That does not sound *unremarkable* to me.

A core part of my job was assessing the value of things, whether they are
assets or companies. To do this, to determine the *value* of something, there
is no end to valuation methodologies that you can employ, ranging from

looking at the cash flows the asset can generate in the future to comparing it to a similar asset that is comparable based on its characteristics. But while you can always conduct the theoretical desktop exercise to come up with a quantitative figure (and come up with ten different numbers to answer the same question), at the end of the day, one must find a willing buyer or seller who is willing to pay you or buy from you the asset at a certain price. If I set aside my financial theory, *the price that someone is willing to pay for something* can very often be used as a proxy to discuss the value of that business. Any of us who have bought or sold a house would be aware that regardless of any 'comparable estimates' based on location, bedrooms, or similar houses, at the end of the day, what someone offers to pay for that house could very well be what it is worth.

Jesus, the Son of God, was willing to give up his life and pay the price for my life. If the price paid to ransom my life is the blood of God Himself, what does that say about my value?

Daughter, that means you are priceless.

And yet, when I hear words that contradict that scripture or thoughts that come into my mind questioning who I am, I have not, in turn, rebuked that word, declaring that it was not true.

My second misstep was an over-reliance on my ability to map out a course for my life and career. To achieve, through mostly my strength, open doors. It is natural to be disappointed when you don't get something you want, but instead of allowing for the possibility that God probably had something better in store for me, I started to lose faith and think that perhaps He was only interested in meeting my needs; not my wants, desires or dreams. The ultimate insult, as if He was not a Father who delighted in being generous with his daughter, but instead a meager thrifty father who only gave the bare minimum.

"Trust in the Lord and do good; dwell in the land and enjoy safe pasture. Take delight in the Lord, and he will give you the desires of your heart." – Psalm 37:3-4

Daughter, when you started to crawl and then, shortly afterward, walk and run around the house, we realized we had to step up our game in babyproofing the house. It was done in stages, more to keep up with you than the recommended approach of doing it before you discovered a hazard. One particular achievement of yours was to one day open the drawer which contained all the cutlery and specifically the chopping knives, which necessitated that we add one of those locks to the drawers which prevents you from opening the drawer unless the clasp is pinched and removed; a difficult maneuver for the toddler and apparently some dads.

But because we were somewhat reactionary in our approach, by the time we added the lock to the drawer, you already knew that you could open that drawer. If we had done it beforehand, perhaps you may never have questioned its ability to open in the first place. But as it were, you knew it could open, and only that you did not know why it wouldn't open now. You would spend endless hours putting your entire body weight on the drawer, pulling hard, even getting your fingers stuck in the gap sometimes, hoping that with the pinch of those little fingertips, you might be able to pry open the drawer. Eventually, you would cry out of frustration and anger.

But it remains shut until I open it.

I wonder if that is what we look like to God when we try to open doors that He has not opened for us yet. How He must look on us, trying to open a door that is not the best door for us, that may even contain danger or harm, but so convinced that it needs to be opened.

One of my new, constant prayers is for God to protect me from myself. I pray that He will close doors that I might be trying to push through if it is not His will for my life. I have made the mistake of barging through doors not meant for me in the past, and I want to avoid a repeat performance. I'm not sure if you feel the same way, but sometimes I feel like I am my own worst enemy.

Thankfully, after much prayer and reflection, I understood I was supposed to stay put and bloom where I was. It would only be a matter of months before the reason would become clear to me, as I did not have the foresight to see what the weaver was able to see. In the meantime, God allowed these circumstances to do surgery on my heart. Eventually, by the time my next step became clearer, I was a different person. My circumstances had not changed at all, but after flailing around for months, facing some harsh truths, the real change was in my attitude. I used to wonder why God allowed such a waste of my time and energy, but now I know that it was not to change my circumstances (or even job) but to change and grow me.

So, I obeyed. Despite so much well-meaning advice from friends and colleagues, I stopped looking around and decided to stay put with my head down and work as hard as possible. I would have one of the best years of my career, even having spent a third of it away on maternity leave. If I knew how the next twelve months would play out when I received that call in December, I might have saved myself so much time, emotional energy, anxiety, and hair. If I had gotten my way trying to make career moves, I would have missed out on one of my career's most enjoyable, challenging, and rewarding years. And worse, as I will share in the following letter, I would not have been in a position to embark on an even more exciting adventure.

As an aside, I must make a mental note to one day, as a hiring manager, hire more mothers or mothers coming back from maternity leave. If it is anything like my personal experience, there is nothing like months of changing diapers and on-call feedings to give you renewed vigor and enthusiasm for your job.

We have all heard, '*the grass is always greener on the other side,*' and you may have even heard my preferred modification to that quote; '*the grass is greener where you water it.*' I would go one step further to say perhaps it was high time I learned that unless God very specifically opens a door and tells me to go through it (more on that later), I should stay on my exact patch of grass and water it, put soil, plant flowers or whatever else we can do in a patch of grass. Maybe this was the point of all that we went through in 2021, to learn to stay put until God opened a door for me and not to rush ahead of Him.

The doom of gloom of 2021 eventually turned into what would be a banner year. Things were looking up, and some amazing doors were opening up in my career.

And then, my husband got a call.

9. faith in action

By the time the end of the year rolled around, it was my husband's turn to think about his next job; this time because my department had helped the Company substantially divest all the business he supported. There was one opportunity, but it would involve a major relocation halfway around the world. At the same time, doors were opening for me right where we were, and in all honesty, I had very little motivation to go anywhere other than possibly to a new address as the renovations on our house continued to drag on. We had also opened our home to a regular small group gathering, and we especially loved leading and serving those couples in our church in this new way and were equally blessed in return. As far as I was from my parents, and as sad as I was that they missed so much of their daughter's pregnancy and their first grandchild's first year of life, I particularly loved being close to my sister, where we were both at least in the same continent for the first time since 2008.

And yet, the events I would describe in *WIFE* would lead me to pen down an impossible declaration of faith about my relationship, my job, my finances, and even another daughter.

Within two weeks of that declaration, my husband got a call saying the job in the Middle East was his if he wanted it.

It should have been a no-brainer, and I suppose for my husband, it was. And even I had to consider that I would be much closer to my parents, who had missed out on so much with my daughter during the pandemic. We would have a better quality of life, more support, and the opportunity to build up our savings. I had even told God I didn't think I wanted another child if I had to do it all alone without support. The country was also extraordinarily beautiful, filled with the most wonderful people, and considered one of the safest countries in the world. So frankly, in terms of an impossibly comprehensive list of needs I had been pestering Him with constantly, this should have been the answer to all. Except, there was still one thing on the list that was missing, and that was enough to make me hesitate.

I had already given up my friends once, a life I had built over fifteen years, being able to visit my parents via a 4-hour flight anytime I wanted or in an emergency, to travel halfway around the world from Singapore to Houston. At the time, I knew it was the right thing to do for our family, sensed God's will in that decision, and even received independent affirmation to ease the doubts in my heart. But at least then, I still had my job and career with a company I loved. This time around, I may have to give that up as well. Taking yet more time out of the workforce would surely doom me to a different life path than I had envisioned, possibly costing me all upward trajectory on my career, this time for good. Everyone knows about the statistics of women in their thirties dropping like flies out of the workforce; I never expected to be one of the statistics myself.

I naturally questioned the source of this good fortune. Was it really from God? It looked like a 'great' thing, but we were serving in a church in Houston and felt we had more to offer in terms of ministry and service. And surely the stress of potentially losing a job or moving continents can't be good for pregnancy prospects. My husband's family also lived in the same city, and a move would mean we would be far from them, a critical support system for any young couple with a toddler and a baby.

If there was ever a moment to seek wisdom and direction from God, this was it. Something could look great on the surface, but only He can let me know if it is the right door and opportunity for all of us. I am so grateful for all the times I have been able to tap into his promise, which says, "I will instruct you and teach you in the way you should go; I will counsel you with my eye upon you" (Psalm 32:8). And so, we decided to postpone the decision for a weekend, go to church on Sunday as usual, engage in undistracted praise and worship and spend time with God together. In my heart, I would say I was not optimistic that I would come to peace with the decision and just hoped for some unity between us as we made the decision either way. As you may have guessed from the humorous and fictional *Guardian Angels in the Meeting Room* scene in the introduction, God was about to give us a big hint in a very obvious way. I suppose when the decision is a pretty drastic one, only the obvious would do when it comes to someone as skeptical as me. It seemed I had my answer; the open door was definitely from God, and He wanted me to say yes.

And yet, I still had one unresolved big, fat question mark, a childish whisper; '*but what about me, God?* I expected the usual promises to comfort me; "The blessing of the Lord brings wealth, without painful toil for it." (Proverbs 10:22); "That the Lord may grant the desires of my heart" (Psalms 20:4); That "God has plans to prosper me and not to harm me, plans to give me a hope and a future" (Jeremiah 29:11), but I had more questions than comfort.

But from my vantage point, I could not see how these promises could materialize for me in this situation. I wanted another child, but I had hoped to do it while still pursuing my aspirations, and my dreams felt like they were further away than ever. I had tried staying at home, and while the first four to five months was a crucial recovery period postpartum, that last sixth month felt like a prison. Is God still trying to do a work in me to change my identity or maybe give me a new dream to hold onto? So many questions to God, but repeatedly, only one answer;

"And without faith it is impossible to please God, for anyone who comes to Him must believe that he exists and that he rewards those who earnestly seek Him." - Hebrews 11:6

I had always thought of myself as someone with great faith. After all, I had witnessed God bring me through some miraculous circumstances even to where I am today, even providing for me through famines. Was He not able to change time itself so that a year that should be a write-off, coming back from maternity leave, was a year of great success? St. Teresa of Avila once said, *"You pay God a compliment when you ask great things of Him."* I was humbled here to consider that perhaps I did not have as much faith in God as I thought, at least not in every aspect of my life. I had not been asking for great things from God, only for things I could visualize or imagine with my limited vision. I had to reckon that what I did not have as much faith in was not his ability to do whatsoever He willed but the very nature of his generosity, his willingness to lavish blessings upon his children. I was putting him in a box with boundaries I could visualize and accept as pragmatic and reasonable.

But here is where Hebrews 11:6 offers us some guidance. I had always paid attention to the first part of that sentence, that we must have faith that He exists, but I rarely reflected on the last part of the verse; *"and that He rewards those who earnestly seek Him."* That was not just about having faith in who He is but in his very nature. It sounds like the same faith my daughter has in me when she cries out to me from her crib in the middle of the night, when she is hungry or thirsty, or even bored; she knows I will always come. She knows I will always meet her needs. Every single time. She doesn't think to herself, 'maybe this time Mummy won't help me' or 'she will not give me food when I am hungry,' or 'she doesn't think I need to eat.' Of course not! She asks, every time, expecting to receive. No wonder Jesus told us to be like little children in our faith!

The more I thought about it, the more I liked the idea that I could please God! Isn't it amazing that the God of the universe could receive *pleasure* from something I could do? Pleasure is so much more intimate and familial than just approval. Approval is given by authorities. Pleasure is experienced in the presence of a relationship. I see this every day in my daughter, who when she discovers something that makes us laugh, does it repeatedly with obvious enjoyment. Or when she gives us a hug or a kiss or strokes my hair, only because we 'coo and aah' with satisfaction, not because she particularly wants to. But it brings *her* pleasure and enjoyment to see *my* pleasure, the person she so dearly loves in this world. I loved the thought that I could bring that kind of pleasure to our Father, who is so generous and kind and compassionate and loving with me. All I had to do was believe in who He is and have faith that He wants to reward his children who seek Him.

So, who was God? With my tiny little human mind, I could not comprehend who God is, but He has revealed Himself to me through the times and continues to do so every day through scripture.

I know He desires all of us to have known Him, have a relationship and be with Him in eternity. To this end, He gave us his only Son, Jesus, to save us. I could not fathom giving up one of my daughters to save the other. I would rather die myself. I suppose, in a way, that is what God did, with his son, Jesus, also God, dying for us. I know He has come through for me time and time again through miraculous provision, even as He sees me faithfully tithing over the decades, remaining true to his word that our barns will be overflowing no matter what goes on around us. In my lowest, darkest moments, I know He has been kneeling there with me, holding me, comforting me, always by my side, never leaving me. I have seen Him guide my steps, gently but firmly, giving me wisdom whenever I ask for it, whether for a problem at work or on a relational matter. He has shown that He is generous, forgiving, passionate in pursuit, gentle and as refreshing as a raindrop on a hot summer day, as strong and protective as a ten-thousand-man army.

But one of my favorite things about Him is shared in the passage Matthew 7:11, "If you, then, though you are evil, know how to give good gifts to your children, how much more will your Father in heaven give good gifts to those who ask Him!"

With a start, I realized I had been undercutting my prayers in a seriously detrimental way by trying not to ask for too much. But now I believe my God loves it when I ask for too much because what is too much, too impossible, too difficult for God? Asking in itself becomes an act of praise and worship, acknowledging his magnificence and sovereignty over all the universe! Would the God who created me down to every atom of my being not know my hopes and dreams? My gifts and talents? My passions and desires? He wishes to give us the Godly desires of our hearts! Did He not instruct us to be productive with our gifts and talents and honor Him with the work of our hands?

More significantly, this was perhaps the biggest opportunity I have had to step out in faith blindly, not knowing what was on the other side, with nothing *but* faith and trust in God. Blind trust is the kind of trust my daughter has in me. I could not help but think about Isaac, who (in Genesis 26:23-25) went to Beersheba, encountered God, built an altar, pitched his tent, and *only then* instructed his servants to dig a well, without which He wouldn't be able to plant Himself there. Faith in God first, provision afterward.

So, I prayed an impossible prayer. A job that satisfies, invigorates, stimulates, and maximizes my capabilities. Time to spend with my family but also a smooth pregnancy and restful maternity break. To be a mother to my daughter and a wife to my husband. Time to finish writing this book. I felt God would need to give me 48 hours in a day to make all this happen.

I'm sure any working mother or some of my friends who are full-time moms and housewives would agree.

But if He wants my faith, He can have my faith! The ball is in His court now.

I had spent most of my life with my hands firmly on the steering wheel, taking input from God, who I allowed to sit in the passenger seat or if I was being honest, a lot of times in the back seat. In a proverbial 'Jesus, take the wheel' situation, it was time for me to hop into the back seat and be chauffeured, resting in Him. I was tired of networking, striving to figure it out for myself, and solving an equation that I felt was missing a critical variable. I just wanted to rest, and more importantly, to *rest in Him* and see what He can do for once if I let Him have full control and not interfere.

Daughter, you can take it for what it's worth, but in my experience and opinion, the most important networking relationship you can have in your career is with God. Yes, all the other relationships are beneficial, but I believe without that most important relationship of all, your biggest champion, your biggest supporter, the one who knows your innermost being, capabilities, desires, passions, skills, talents, gifts, is uselessly benched, relegated to being an observer, not an active mover and shaker. On the other hand, if He is in control, the sky is the limit. I love this promise of his;

"What, then, shall we say in response to these things? If God is for us, who can be against us? He who did not spare his own Son, but gave him up for us all how will he not also, along with him, graciously give us all things?" -Romans 8:31-32

This verse is often misquoted out of context. I believe it is not about giving us a Ferrari if we ask for it (perhaps I am just upset that I can only drive vehicles that fit two car seats in the back for the foreseeable future). I believe our generous, loving father desires to give us things that will allow us to live a grace-filled, fulfilling life before being with Him in eternity. This is not everything we ask for. After all, if I opened that drawer my daughter wants to get into, the one with the chopping knives, that is hardly a good thing for her. But I believe this is everything we need to live a purpose-driven, generous, peace-filled, grace-enabled life according to his word and promises. Yes, that includes opening the right doors to maximize our God-given potential. And so, I dreamed, prayed, and hoped for big things.

In the (many) months that followed, I had to encourage myself in prayer many times. Almost eight months is a long time to wait, though I suppose a minuscule amount of time compared to some of our other long-standing prayers spanning decades. I was often reminded of Peter, who was called out of the boat by Jesus. Peter gets a lot of criticism, but he did step out of that boat in faith and legitimately walked on water for a bit. But that is not the encouraging bit. I love what happens next. Even Peter, who had *just* been walking on water, looked around, saw the storm, became fearful, and started to sink. Jesus immediately reached out to grab Peter and put him on the boat to ensure he was okay. He didn't stand there admonishing Peter, saying, "you just did it; you can do it again! Come on! Get back up!". No, Jesus loved Peter the way He loves us and knows when we need some help, even with our faith. He asked, "Oh ye of little faith, why did you doubt?" But He only asked that *after* rescuing Peter. In those months of waiting, I needed a helping hand to build myself up in faith again, to remember what was promised. In every season of waiting, I encourage you, daughter, to keep returning to the promise and not take for granted that a moment of great faith is enough to see you through long waiting periods.

Looking back, those months were a gift.

When we are asked to think about the most valuable asset on earth, we often think of money.

But I heard of an important question that we could ask ourselves; "Would you be willing to switch places with a billionaire who was pushing a hundred?" Most said the answer would be a "No". Is that surprising? Why? Because no amount of money ever bought a second of time.

If not for the pandemic, the decision to keep my daughter at home with a nanny might have seemed like a financially foolish decision, albeit one that we had the privilege of being able to make; I know that is not the case for most women. As it was, it became a necessity, and my daughter, whether it was the pandemic, my mother visiting for an extended time, or our move internationally, managed to dodge daycare till she was well past eighteen months. At the same time, most of us were relegated to working from home, which meant that even when I went back to work full time, I could pop in and see her during lunch breaks or even hear her laughter and giggles as I went about my day. I had talked about God's financial generosity in our lives and how I believe tithing faithfully helped unlock greater levels of blessing, but if you ask me, that time of being present in my daughter's life was probably the greatest gift He could have ever given me. To this day, I am so thankful that He has placed me in a company that allowed flexible working arrangements, which was something I desperately needed in that season in my life. And I thank Him for knowing how deeply I desired to keep my daughter in the house in these early years and generously providing a way. Now, I can't wait to return to the office because an active two-year-old who can open locked doors has effectively killed that season of my life, but I am going back with no regrets.

Shortly after my great declaration of faith, I would become pregnant again in January. We would be selling our house and moving inter-continentally with an eighteen-month-old toddler while I was going through my first trimester, which proved much more difficult than my first pregnancy. I had months of morning sickness and fatigue compared to the breezy two weeks of nausea I enjoyed with my first baby. Once we moved, my daughter and I would take turns becoming sick for almost two months as we both acclimatized to her starting daycare and a new environment. If I had been in the middle of an intense deal during this period, I know I would not have been able to cope. As it was, I could work flexibly, with reduced deal activity, while I waited for my next role. This book certainly would not have happened without these few months. I had procrastinated on writing many times for all the noblest reasons, but like Jonah, who was swallowed up by a whale to make sure he obeyed God in what he was directed to do, I have also felt somewhat as if I am inside the belly of the whale until I finish writing this book. Next time, I will be much more expeditious when He tells me to do something. Perhaps my favorite perk during this season of waiting was that I got to spend some quality time with my daughter before her sister showed up, a period I am sure will be a difficult adjustment for her. On my deathbed, or maybe as soon as a moody teenager is shut away in her room, I know I will never regret this extra time I spent with my daughter.

Daughter, when it comes to our workplaces, one of the greatest blessings that God bestows on us, even, I think, more than our jobs, is great colleagues and great leaders. It's commonly accepted that *"people leave bosses, not jobs."* But the reverse is also very much true. The leaders that were in my life during this season have, I feel, set the gold standard for the kind of support that I would one day hope to give my team should I ever be in a similar position. Much like the last time I hoped for a dream job, a job materialized out of thin air, one that checked all of my boxes, and perhaps even a few that I did not know should be in the list. As I sit here, penning these words, all I can think of is a line from one of my favorite movies, *Facing the Giants;*

"David, you tell me, what is impossible for God?"

"Nothing."

Nihara Guruge

leader

Nihara Guruge

10. breaking all the rules

I didn't grow up thinking I was an underdog or had some disadvantage in life. That was something that would be hammered into me by the world much, much later on. I grew up as the ethnic majority, albeit in a developing country, in an all-girl catholic school, in a household where my mother worked for most of my life. Little in that experience told me I was not as smart or as capable as my male peers. Growing up, my sister and I played squash professionally. The core training group often ended up on the court together, consisting of two of the top male players in the country, along with my sister and me. They were stronger than us, but we could certainly give them a run for their money, occasionally even outlasting them on the court or being just as fast with our reflexes. No one expected less of us because we were girls.

At home, it was accepted that we continue with our studies to the best of our ability. Marriage was not expected of us, at least until we finished university. A few years after graduation, my lack of progress (or even effort) in that area would prompt my very South Asian dad to ask me if I 'needed help.' Every few years, my sister and I would suffer through occasional, somewhat passive-aggressive, 'so and so's son is very eligible' until we both finally tied the knot. This was all against the backdrop of a country that boasted of Queens dating back thousands of years, or the first female prime minister in the world, or even a female president in present times (who *did* lose an eye due to a terrorist attack, but all things considered, fared better than her predecessor who gave his life to a similar attack). All this is to say that the glass ceiling was not a concept that had entered my consciousness.

This all changed when I moved to Singapore. For the first time, I was an ethnic minority, but other than the occasional dash of casual racism, I did not directly feel unwelcome in any way at my university. But this would be the first time I would realize just how much wealth there was in the world and how little of it is accessible to many. More than gender or race, social class seems to most accurately represent the cards you are dealt in life, able to either overcome or magnify any other obstacle on life's path.

I was the elder daughter of a middle-class family in a poor country. My mother achieved what was considered normal in her time: a high school education, marriage to her first love at the age of twenty, and the birth of her two daughters, all by her early twenties. She then stepped into a career consisting of several jobs as a secretary or executive assistant, which only ended in 2019 upon her retirement. My father took a somewhat more unorthodox path, with his education followed by the Air Force (where he met said mother, who was his boss's daughter, the boss being the Air Force Commander himself; needless to say, 'spunk' is not lacking in the gene pool), a few National Championships for Badminton & Squash, followed by a foray into various business administration roles. Financially, and I will get into this more later, we had just about enough to meet our needs with the occasional period of extreme difficulty and stress due to unemployment. When I came to Singapore, I did so with no connections that could help me get a job when I graduated, and given that school accommodations are not provided during the break, I could only afford to stay in the country for an internship because a friend from college let me bunk in at her family home for the holidays. If I am ever in a position to affect change, one of the first things I would do is to provide a living wage to interns, without which employers naturally shrink the talent pool to a privileged few who could afford to work for low or no salary.

You might be wondering where I am going with this and why I have left this letter till the end. In some ways, daughter, this is the most important letter of them all.

Many have heard the story of David and Goliath, how the small David valiantly took on the giant Goliath, delivering the kingdom with what one can only describe as the bull's eye of the century. But I often wonder at the years David spent as a shepherd. He was not the oldest son and was unlikely to inherit his father's business. He also had a lot of time on his hands, as I'm sure the sheep rarely talked back. Did he have visions and dreams of his future? Were they of starting his own business? Increasing the herd? Of taking over the family business? One thing I do surmise, he did not dream of being a king. At the ripe old age of thirty-five, I have now spent most of my life acutely aware of all the supposed disadvantages afforded me. At different points in my life, I wished my family had more money, that I was a man and not a woman in this world, or to be a different race that might afford me more advantages, or at the very least, supposedly fewer *dis*advantages. Frankly, to walk into a room and not have to prove that you have a right to be there as much as the next guy sitting next to you would, in itself, be a welcome breath of fresh air. What is perhaps even more exhausting is that every day there seems to be one more label out there, one more box, or one more identifier to segregate us, define us, or determine just how well we should be doing or how easy or difficult the path ahead for us would be. At the end of the day, it all seems to point to one of the biggest questions humans, and especially women, are destined to seek to answer; *Who am I?*

"The spirit himself testifies with our spirit that we are God's children. Now, if we are children, then we are heirs- heirs of God and co-heirs with Christ." - Romans 8:16-17

Technically, my daughter is ethnically mixed (although she looks like a carbon copy of her dad), as my husband is Black and I am Sinhalese. But one of the biggest concerns the four grandparents had when she was born, both my parents, who are Sri Lankan, and my husband's parents, who are American, was how our daughter would learn of her identity and culture. My parents were concerned that if she grew up in America, she would not know of her Sri Lankan heritage, language or culture, or history. My husband's parents were similarly concerned that if I did not immerse her with a sufficient cultural education, she would not know what it would mean to be a (half) black woman in America and all that it entails. My husband and I seem somewhat unconcerned, and laissez-faire in our approach and response to this very important topic which probably did not assuage anyone's fears or concerns. Given careers and chosen international lifestyles, I suspect my daughters will spend much of their life trying to understand where they fit into the world.

Perhaps you are starting to guess why I kept this letter until the end.

"Who am I?" was a question I've had to examine throughout my life, but perhaps never as much as when I added on 'mother' on top of the existing

'wife,' 'employee,' 'daughter,' or any number of other roles we hold. You may have heard the following story before;

There once was a philosophy professor who was giving a lecture. In front of him, he had a big glass jar, a pile of rocks, a bag of small pebbles, a tub of sand, and a bottle of water. He started by filling up the jar with the big rocks, and when they reached the rim of the jar, he held it up to the students and asked them if the jar was full. They all agreed there was no more room to put the rocks in because it was full.

"Is it full?" he asked.

He then picked up the bag of small pebbles and poured these into the jar. He shook the jar so that the pebbles filled the space around the big rocks. "Is the jar full now?" he asked. The group of students all looked at each other and agreed that the jar was now completely full.

"Is it really full?" he asked.

The professor then picked up the tub of sand. He poured the sand between the pebbles and the rocks, and once again, he held up the jar to his class and asked if it was full. Once again, the students agreed that the jar was full.

"Are you sure it's full?" he asked.

He finally picked up a bottle of water and tipped the water into the jar until it soaked up in all the remaining space in the sand. The students laughed.

The professor explained that the jar of rocks, pebbles, sand, and water represents everything in one's life.

The metaphor is clear. The rocks, pebbles, sand, and water represent competing priorities in our lives, the rocks being the most important and the sand or pebbles being less important. Depending on which version of the story you hear, there are different lists of things that can qualify as 'rocks,' 'pebbles,' or 'sand.' But most of all, I think the rocks represent not just those things that are most important to us but also the very same things that often tend to define us.

Some women can seamlessly transition into motherhood, but as I shared with you earlier in the book, I was not one of those women because it was not something I had pursued most of my life. Not only was I now faced with trying to stuff a pretty significant rock into what felt like an already full jar, but I was also going through a season of breaking down and rebuilding where my jar was being shaken out, broken, put back together, with all the other rocks looking a little bit more different by the time I was going back to work after maternity leave.

Before I became a mother, I was fortunate to have had supportive parents and, subsequently, a supportive partner who did not at any point tell me that I could not or should not pursue my goals. Granted, my mother did waver, occasionally cautioning against high-stress jobs and their potential to impact fertility, but it was rarely a point that was pressed too hard as she undoubtedly thought it would fall on deaf ears. It was certainly not an effective tactic for someone who did not even want children in the first place. The various rocks in my life were clear and rarely in conflict with each other. I had comfortably defined myself as a go-getter, driven, ambitious, passionate, and fearless. Even marriage was optional, as I was perfectly content to be single for the foreseeable future.

That reality was to be completely dismantled when I became a mother. My company afforded me a generous maternity break, so when I was ready to return to work, I was truly ready. And yet, even when my baby was six months old, the idea of having her away from me for ten to twelve hours of the day felt deeply abhorrent to me, triggering guilt that I did not expect. I know it is the reality of many working mothers, but for the first time in my life, it was enough to make me question if I am truly on the right path in life. Of all the legacies we leave behind when we die, our children tend to be one of the ones with an impact lasting for generations. It's an important job to do right.

For the first time, I was forced to ask myself, 'are the things I so deeply aspired for myself *good* and *pure* and *of God?*' I was not sure. After all, I had always confidently claimed that I was *not* the 'maternal type,' keeping a healthy distance from all children and babies below the age of seven until that moment in my life. And yet, here I was, so deeply in tune with my baby's needs, so in love with her, and possibly a great Montessori teacher given a chance. Sufficiently 'maternal' enough to shock all my friends and even my husband. It was enough to make me question if I even knew myself at all, or worse, if I had become a different person in motherhood.

When I thought that I would have to give up my career and be renegaded to a full-time mother and housewife, to put it bluntly, I lost it. To put it less bluntly and a bit kindlier, I went through an identity crisis. Here was this door that God had opened so clearly that I had to go through it, but it might involve stripping away the very things I held so closely tied to who I was, or at least, as I had defined who I was. As we speak, there is a global movement to self-declare aspects of our identity, such as gender, sexuality, ethnicity, nationality, etc., that we believe will significantly impact who we are and how we show up for work. I applaud this effort as I believe that without objective, unbiased data, we will never be able to solve some of the questions of bias and inequality in the system. But is that who I am? A Sri Lankan born and bred/Singaporean/American-based, Asian, heterosexual female? A woman with a career? Wife and mother? A daughter and sister? Christian? Feminist? A Christian-Feminist?

But if these things, which are so fluid and ever-changing in life, define who I am, then what happens when you start to peel off those labels? Losing or changing jobs and careers and losing loved ones is part of the constant change in life. Even when God was pointing out to me that I was holding onto something too tightly, when He was telling me to let go for some purpose that was still unknown, I was struggling, refusing to let go. Parenting a toddler makes you realize that they sometimes seem to defy the laws of physics; nothing makes me question my strength as much as when I try to pry something out of my two-year-old's hands. But I have a lot in common with that toddler sometimes, clutching to things so hard that I refuse to let go, even when I'm told to do so by my generous Father who only wants what is good for me.

I've heard time and time again the saying that 'we all worship something.' In the ancient days, even after God freed the Israelites from Egypt, in Exodus 32, we see how quickly the Israelites gave up on Moses' return from Mount Sinai and created an idol of gold for themselves or even later worshipping other false gods who their neighbors worshiped. This is perhaps unsurprising as the Bible alludes to the fact that we were created for worship, for a relationship with God.

"You are worthy, our Lord and God, to receive glory and honor and power, for you created all things, and by your will they were created and have their being." – Revelations 4:11

Worship is an innate need, even a siren call to our souls. Perhaps that is why that nothing makes me feel as fulfilled, satisfied and content, as when my arms are raised up in worship. Unfortunately, this means that in the absence of God, we are very much tempted to create something to worship. What is frightening is that these days the idols aren't in the form of a golden calf, or always in towering temples full of animal demigods. That would be obvious and much easier to deal with. If an idol is anything we place above our wholehearted devotion and obedience to God, our father, and his son, Jesus Christ, then the list is endless; possessions, careers, comfort, our bodies, or even religiosity at the expense of dishonoring God and his basic commandments to love God and to love people even above our preferences and rights. With self-care (and not the kind of rest and meditation Jesus modeled, more like shopping sprees and cancelling relationships) becoming a trending topic in recent times, often a reason to forego other-care, the type of sacrificial living embodied by Jesus, I think 'self' has become yet another idol of our times.

We spend an extraordinary amount of our time on earth working. If so, I could be forgiven for caring about what I do, the work of my hands. I wanted it to be exciting and not just something I did to pay the bills or pass the time. But my idol was that my identity is tied so closely to my career and achievements, the affirmation and recognition I get through it, that I wasn't clear anymore if I was doing it because it was the task given to me by God, my assignment on earth, or was it an addiction in and of itself feeding into a sense of worth and pride with every milestone. *Why do I do what I do?* There was only one way to be sure: to let go and take that step I was being asked to take. At best, I will receive a positive confirmation from God that I am where I am supposed to be, and He will work out my next steps for me. At worst, I will be able to start the process of culling an idol, stepping out of the rat race, and resetting and redefining my purpose on earth. The latter was scary, and my heart was not in it, as I desperately loved what I did for a living, but it was necessary.

One of my favorite books to read is C.S. Lewis' *Screwtape Letters[1]*, in which Screwtape (a higher-ranked experienced demon) is mentoring Wormwood, who is likely one of the minions in Satan's dominion. The Enemy who Screwtape often references is God. Their demonic goal, of course, is to capture the human soul for eternity. In one such letter, he writes;

"Do not be deceived, Wormwood. Our cause is never more in danger than when a human, no longer desiring, but still intending, to do our Enemy's will, looks round upon a universe from which every trace of Him seems to have vanished and asks why he has been forsaken, and still obeys."- C. S. Lewis, The Screwtape Letters.

Does this not remind you of Jesus? If so, does anything sound more Christ-like than doing God's will even when you don't *feel* like it? Or even when you can't *see* God, let alone *feel* Him?

Daughter, Christianity is not for the faint-hearted.

But how can you do God's will, trust his purpose for our lives, and trust Him when He asks us to let go of dreams or plans, or that He wants good for us if we don't even see or know how He views *us?*

Actually, we *do* know! We just choose to ignore it because it's much easier to define ourselves with things we see, like our careers or possessions (so much easier to compare if we are 'doing well' or, more importantly, 'doing better than..'!), how we look (after all, isn't the body the temple of the Holy Spirit?) or even our families, relationships or past hurts. But none of these things show up as a good measure of our worth in the Bible, and that is a very good thing because the only constant among all these identifiers is that they change. We lose jobs. We have our reputations smeared by one piece of gossip (that could even be untrue). We lose loved ones. We all age and lose that waistline or hair. Wounds heal. Some seem to have it all, and some seem to have nothing.

If you struggle with your eyesight and have had to seek out a prescription for spectacles, you would know that, in general, the further away from zero is the number on your prescription, the worse your eyesight and the more vision correction (stronger prescription) you need. I would propose that when it comes to your identity, we need to be as far away as possible, thirty thousand, forty thousand, a hundred thousand feet away, if necessary, to stop looking at ourselves through the human lens and all its identifiers, and to look at ourselves through God's eyes. As an added benefit, you will look at everyone with the same lens at that kind of altitude. Even your spouse who keeps forgetting that one thing all the time, your child who seems so determined to disobey you, your colleague who talked about you behind your back, your employee who can't seem to deliver those results, your leader whose policies you disagree with, or a president who you find morally repugnant.

God says I am loved, and no one in the history of the earth or its future has my DNA. In fact, I was so loved by God that He sacrificed his Son to bring me back to Him (John 3:16, NIV).

I am chosen not just to be His daughter but to be a co-heir with Christ, to inherit his kingdom for all eternity, and I am uniquely chosen for a specific calling and purpose in my life. I am forgiven of all my past and future mistakes and sins because God has adopted me through Jesus, who I have accepted in my life. I try to do my best to live my life worthy of my title and crown, and I will keep falling short for the rest of my life, but that is okay because it does not change my position or status as an adopted daughter of God. I am a member of God's household (Ephesians 2:19).

My father blesses me and provides for me (2 Corinthians 9:8). He delights in me (Zephaniah 3:17).

Wow. This, then, is the answer to *Who I am*. Faced with this truth, how can any job title or pay slip, or trophy ever compete?

There are so many more passages that will be a balm upon your soul, and daughter, I encourage you to read the Bible and be on a journey of discovery to see what God is telling you through his great love letter.

If you must be labeled or put into a box, that is a much better box to check, in my opinion.

When I started working, I began to straighten my hair chemically. I have naturally thick, wavy hair, which looks great when styled well but terrible when working in one of the most humid places on earth, like Singapore or Houston. Straight hair meant I spent virtually no time every morning on it, which allowed me to sleep for those extra few minutes. I also (foolishly) read many articles and research on how straight hair was perceived as more competent in the workplace due to abject workplace biases. It seemed like everyone in Singapore had beautiful straight black hair, and frankly, after suffering through enough 'jokes' about my hair during my university days, I just wanted to fit in. It would be a decade of periodic chemical hair straightening and routine exposure to harmful chemicals before I finally started to want to live with my natural hair texture again. Other things, like the color of my skin, my gender, or my background, are less easily changed with a Keratin treatment.

Now I know better; confidence is not about who you are. It's about who you believe in.

If you believe in yourself, great! But you, more than anyone else, know your limitations.

"Yours, Lord, is the greatness and the power and the glory and the majesty and the splendor, for everything in heaven and earth is yours.

Yours, Lord, is the kingdom; you are exalted as head over all. Wealth and honor come from you; you are the ruler of all things. In your hands are strength and power to exalt and give strength to all." -1 Chronicles 29:11-12

If, however, my confidence is in God who rules over all things, to whom the structures and processes of this earth are subservient, and *that* God is for me, fights for me, ordains my paths *because of who He says I am*, then I can start to step out of the little leagues and start to play in the major leagues. David was a harpist, the youngest of eight sons. Nothing in his resume said King of Israel. And yet, that was the purpose that God saw for his life. Through his obedience, starting with just throwing one stone, he eventually became a king of a nation.

Daughter, if you want confidence, do not look around for it in anyone or anything. Do not even look inside of yourself. Look up.

As I write this, I have no clarity of how my life will look in five, ten, or twenty years. But I am brimming with confidence. When I penned this letter, I did not even have a job offer, although that has changed since then. I know who God is and who I am, and I know God has a purpose for my life that I can fulfill as long as I listen to Him and walk with Him. And I know enough about Him to know that He is not for mediocrity, or 'just enough'. He is an all-consuming, overwhelmingly passionate, exciting God. And He has wired me a certain way with unique gifts, and He knows what is *my* best life and is actively working all things out for my good. That gives me all the confidence in the world.

I started this letter saying that I was not an underdog, and I concluded the letter stating the same. By all that we see around us, *I should be*. But if I had all the advantages and privileges of this world, how would I be able to stand here before you and say, "It was God."

If David wasn't so insignificant but a great esteemed warrior, would we be in awe, even today, thousands of years later, of what God did for the Israelites that day? I think not. I have titled this letter 'breaking all the rules' because I have come to realize that with God, we are not playing by the same set of rules. We are not hamsters running on a wheel, destined never to outrun our fate or the statistical probabilistic outcomes for our lives.

"But he said to me, "My grace is sufficient for you, for my power is made perfect in weakness." Therefore I will boast all the more gladly about my weaknesses, so that Christ's power may rest on me. That is why, for Christ's sake, I delight in weaknesses, in insults, in hardships, in persecutions, in difficulties. For when I am weak, then I am strong."– 2 Corinthians 12:9-10

So daughter, don't ever let anyone tell you that you are not good enough. Or that the cards you have been dealt in life mean that you are less likely to be a leader or sit in that boardroom or be a good mother or that you will likely not go on to do great things for God. You have been marked for greatness by God, and I pray that you will know Him and be guided by Him to discover that purpose. With God, all things are possible.

I enjoy coming home and shocking my husband with drastic changes to my hair. The pixie cut of 2017 has been a clear winner to this day, deeply shocking and also conflicting my husband between his trendy, fashion-forward outlook and a desire to see me with long hair, so I certainly make no promises for the future as far as my hair is concerned. But at least I know whatever I choose to do, how I dress, and how I present myself has to do with what brings me enjoyment and joy, and not because I think I need to play by a certain set of rules. Those rules don't apply to children of God.

[1] Lewis, C. S. 2012. *The Screwtape Letters*. C. S. Lewis Signature Classic. London, England: William Collins.

11. a woman at work

Daughter, there is something uniquely precious about you. There is no one else like you, no one else who has had your experiences, your personality, or your character. If you are fortunate enough to be able to bring your whole self to work, your womanhood, your motherhood, and above all, your faith, I believe that can be a great blessing to any workplace or community that you are called into by God. Perhaps most obvious is that you would know that despite the daily temptation to believe otherwise, despite our fleeting emotions trying to mislead us, we know one basic truth; *It is not just about me.* We have a calling to do our tasks dutifully, using our gifts diligently, but we aren't doing it for our glory or fame. We are doing it for God. And we do it with the hope that in all that we do, we can bring glory and honor to the God that we publicly proclaim. In that light, the stranger who cut the queue in the coffee shop is not just an annoyance but a child of God, a soul that is precious to Him. Your team member is not just a warm body to carry their weight in the project deliverable, but a child of God whose well-being and mental health are of utmost importance to Jesus. Your leader is not just a supervisor or manager but someone placed in that position of leadership and authority by God Himself for a purpose. In short, every time we step into our workplaces, we surround ourselves with souls and lives that are precious to God, not headcount or statistics.

Leadership becomes more than managing, supervising, and even promoting, but about deeply caring at a very basic level for souls.

I fall short of this lofty ideal daily, both at home and at work, and can only keep my head up high because I know I am forgiven, and perfection is not expected of me; I will struggle till I die.

There are countless leadership paradigms in the world, and it seems as though every other year, a consulting firm can come up with a new framework or methodology for assessing and measuring leadership potential. But if I were to measure up all the leaders I have had the privilege to follow, the ones that stood out have one common characteristic. *They care.* I suppose it's not going to be a very high-paying consulting report to say that a mark of leadership requires you to be a decent individual who cares about your team; that would be a very short report indeed. Nor does care require a special skill, belief system, or religious ideology.

But I offer you these nuggets to ponder on: If you have allowed your heart to be softened over the years, accepting of the differences between you and your spouse, forgiving and loving them anyway for their unique contributions, no matter how different to your own, you will inevitably have a new perspective when dealing with conflict at work caused by the unique differences among people.

Maybe you have experienced the constant struggle of a mother returning to work, the burden of societal pressure threatening to crush her with expectations of perfection in the home while demanding excellence at work, which could mean that you are best placed to provide a wholly unique level of support to her or her partner in the workplace.

Or if you have developed for yourself a strong conviction of your unique purpose and identity in God, failure and closed doors become stepping stones, allowing you to reach down and pick up a colleague who could be crumbling and encourage them in a whole new way.

Above all, your unique struggles, the things you fear will cripple you at work, can be the source of the greatest empathy and understanding, connecting you to a much wider community than just yourself- if you allow it. The rest of this letter will show just a few areas of my life where that has been the truth.

Be Authentic and Honest

"But the Lord said to Samuel, "Do not look on his appearance or on the height of his stature, because I have rejected him. For the Lord sees not as man sees: man looks on the outward appearance, but the Lord looks on the heart." -1 Samuel 16:7

If anyone ever asks me about the lowest point in my career so far, my response would be immediate. While I was still a graduate analyst, just starting out in the workplace, I had to present the yearly performance of results of the business I supported to the Marketing General Manager of the division. Unfortunately, it was far from a successful presentation due to many reasons, not least because I was delivering extremely bad news. Suffice to say the hour ended with me hastily running into the ladies' restrooms to hide myself in a cubicle and have a self-pitying, embarrassed cry.

I felt like such a complete failure, both in terms of what just happened, how publicly it happened as well as my weakness in this moment.

I carried that incident with me for weeks, if not months before meeting with a senior female leader over lunch, who would later become a much-admired manager, mentor and coach to me. I'm not sure what compelled me to share the incident, but I blurted it out over what I recall was a rather tasteless lunch, and then sat back horrified that I had shared something that made me look so weak and overly sensitive. What happened next changed my view of leadership and female mentoring forever. She shared with me an incident of similar distress that she had encountered early on in her career, without judgement or even advice. In that moment, I did not feel condemned, but understood. More importantly, I felt that I was not alone.

Daughter, please know that you are not alone.

I would not have felt that without this leader being willing to share with me her own personal experience without regard for how it would make her look. We live in a 'fake it till you make it' culture, but as most who have made it would testify, if that is your chosen path, you will find that you never stop faking it. Instead of being the thermometers of our workplace, merely reflecting the temperature of our departments and organizations, let's choose to be thermostats, active ingredients able to change the very temperature of the room that you walk into with your authenticity and honesty. How can you inspire the trust of others, without first trusting them with the truth of who you are? Of your struggles, doubts and insecurities? I promise, I have not met anyone who did have one.

Writing this book was a painful, cringeworthy experience. Even to the end, I kept half-heartedly hoping that perhaps it would not be read by anyone beyond my inner circle, and perhaps it would not be. But daughter, it is important for me to share this with you, because I guarantee that not much, or frankly anything, that you are going through has not been the prior experience of a woman before or beside you. It is our divine duty to lift others up in encouragement and one of the most effective tools we have in our arsenal to do this is having the courage to be authentic and vulnerable about who we are.

Accept the Seasons

After I gave birth to my first daughter, there was one question I received more than any other; "will you go back to work now, or will you quit and stay at home?" I used to complain endlessly to my husband that no one ever seemed to ask *him* that question, which I might have expected to hear in Asia but certainly not in the United States. With a bit more accumulated wisdom and a mere pittance of experience over two years, I am now a tad more forgiving of the question as I realize just how much the little ones need their mother or primary caregiver in those early years. The knowledge that the first three years of an infant's life can have unimaginable and far-reaching impacts on their adult lives, effects that science is just beginning to understand, but perhaps intuitively known to our grandparents and ancestors for eons, softens my heart to the well-meaning question that may otherwise have prickled my sensibilities. Regardless, as you have been on that journey of identity and purpose with me till now, you would have realized that at least as of now, at this point in time, I did not feel called to full-time motherhood. I thank God for that clarity and conviction because it shielded me and softened the enormous guilt I felt when I went back to work, even though I was one of the fortunate few who could continue working from home for over a year after my return from maternity leave. My mother was watching my daughter during one of those months when she took her first step though she kindly pretended not to have observed the milestone. I felt disappointment and guilt that I missed that moment. In fact, guilt threatens to be a constant companion when it comes to being a working mother.

Buy *why* do we feel so much guilt? Are we holding ourselves to a standard of perfection, trying to be perfect career women, perfect mothers, and perfect wives and daughters, all as though we have fifty-six hours in a day? That we want to excel in every responsibility that God has entrusted us with is natural. After all, the Bible says, *"Whatever you do, work at it with all your heart, as working for the Lord, not for human masters, since you know that you will receive an inheritance from the Lord as a reward. It is the Lord Christ you are serving" (Colossians 3:23-24).* Thereby hard work and excellence in all that we do is a given. But the thought of having a portfolio of responsibilities like the Proverbs 31-woman, wife, mother, entrepreneur, tradesman, and household manager, among countless others, makes me want to check myself into a yoga retreat for exhaustion. Frankly, I also find that society goes out of its way to pile on the pressure. Let me give you an example. Thursdays are 'special events' day in my daughter's daycare, which means they frequently dress up as characters for anything and everything ranging from 'career day' to 'today we are all going to dress up as princes and princesses for no apparent reason day.' I am only half ashamed to say that when picking which four days the week my daughter attends nursery, I deliberately avoided the 'fun day.' Frankly, I did not want to spend hours and hours of my free time looking for costumes every other week. I'm sure I could squeeze it into my to-do list if I wanted to, but I did not want to. I take comfort in the fact that she is barely two years old and thus has no consciousness of missing out. Does this make me an imperfect mother? Probably. But I know I'm still a pretty good one, as my daughter is very loved and cared for, so I've had to let go of that self-imposed standard.

Or perhaps it is having to block off my calendar for certain times of the day when I need to do school pick up, drop off, or bedtime in the evenings, and I will have to do so until my daughters pass the infant/toddler phase. I've had to go from being always available at work, even on weekends, to superhumanly juggling conflicting priorities and feel like I am falling short of a 100% commitment at work and home. I can only hope that being present and delivering when I *am* available can make up for even a small part of the time that I cannot be flexible. I have had to make sure that during this period, I work for flexible employers who understand that the output matters and not the ability to keep my seat warm for a certain number of hours of the day.

But most importantly, I have come to realize that *if* we can 'have it all', at best, we need to recognize that 'we can have it all, *but maybe not at the same time'*. In other words, *there are seasons in life.* Ecclesiastes is believed to be written by King Solomon, the wisest and most prosperous man that ever lived, who shares that there is a season for everything in life.

"There is a time for everything,
and a season for every activity under heaven:
a time to be born and a time to die,
a time to plant and a time to uproot,
a time to kill and a time to heal,
a time to tear down and a time to build,
a time to weep and a time to laugh,
a time to mourn and a time to dance,
a time to scatter stones and a time to gather them,
a time to embrace and a time to refrain,
a time to search and a time to give up,
a time to keep and a time to throw away,
a time to tear and a time to mend,
a time to be silent and a time to speak,
a time to love and a time to hate,
a time for war and a time for peace."
- Ecclesiastes 3:1-8

As humans, our concept of time is so linear. We choose to view our lives through the lens of the 'now' and 'past.' But I can't help but wish I could see my life in its entirety and not just as a snapshot in time. Perhaps then I can appreciate that what is true for all of creation and nature is true for us as well; we are all bound by seasons in our life. I can't help but wonder if the many accomplishments of the Proverbs 31 woman was meant to illustrate a lifetime of accomplishments and not just a 'day in the life of.' Perhaps she spent a few years wholly devoted to breastfeeding her children. She spent another year investing in a vineyard. She spent a few more years building up her trade. She spends a few hours every day managing her household (with clearly noted female servants who help her). If she were to compare herself against a different Proverbs 31 woman, perhaps they found themselves in different seasons of life, and it was only at the end of their time that a true measure could be taken as to the worth of the life lived. Perhaps if we accept this and are more forgiving of our own impossible standards, we might be able to let go of the iron grip with which we manage our lives and let God be in control more often. I would certainly love to think that it might just mean that at least there will be fewer of us burning out and leaving the workplace altogether because we tried to do too much at the same time and thought that the shortcoming is with us.

Champion the Good

Daughter, the thing that might make you feel out of place or different might be the best thing about you.

Are you not convinced? Think about this. I think we can all agree that even the most reluctant employer or country acknowledges that a woman who gives birth to a child needs some time off to recover and to tend to the infant. Of course, you see varying degrees of societal acceptance of the task of continuation of humanity and all that it entails. In some countries, mothers get up to years off work, and sometimes fathers do as well. In others, you could be demanded to come back to work six weeks after birth, which anyone who has given birth knows you may not have even stopped bleeding by then or worse, if you have had a cesarian birth, are certainly not fully healed. There is even still a stigma even in some developed countries about taking maternity leave; this toxic thought that becoming a mother must now mean you do not care about having a career at all, pressuring mothers to come back to work before they are ready and work twice as hard as before to prove otherwise. One of my personal favorites is a comment I received when I said I was thinking of not just using my full four-month entitlement but extending it up to six months (a necessity driven by COVID-19 but also my unwillingness to rush back to work at the time given a first-time mother) about my maternity leave being a 'vacation.' A laughable idea to anyone who has taken care of a newborn. And yet, with all this pressure and stigma, it is still accepted that the mother takes time off.

Do you know who invented the idea, advocated, lobbied, and won paid maternity leave for all? A coalition of women, of course.

Unfortunately, making this support universally available to all working mothers or even support for the father or secondary caregiver has much further to go. While there are male leaders who understand and champion the cause, there is still much more encouragement to be given to our sons, husbands, and colleagues to take time off should they wish to do so to support their partners and bond with their children.

Every mother knows just how invaluable that extra pair of hands is in the middle of the night to hold the crying baby after feeding or even to be the safety net and step in when the mother is clearly at her breaking point. Given the extra encouragement needed by even the most well-meaning, supportive husbands and fathers to overcome fears and concerns on their job performance, who better than a wife or a mother who has experienced first-hand the cruciality of their role to give that extra assurance to fathers who wish to take time off that their jobs, their careers, too, are safe. Who better understands the flexibility needed in the workday to share the burden of midafternoon school pick-ups?

Daughter, do not despise and shun your motherhood; it could be the very thing that gives you the empathy to leave a lasting impact on mothers and fathers who step into parenthood after you, leaving a permanent mark on lives as they always remember 'that manager who supported me enough to give me those months with my son and daughter that I will never have again.' Now, that legacy is not washed away by the next quarter's financial results. One thing I am sure of is that a roomful of working mothers will not refer to maternity or paternity leave as vacation and that in itself will be progress.

Believe in His Timing

As I write this, we are in the midst of unusual phenomena in several labor markets whereby there is an ongoing war for talent and resources leading to, for the first time in a long time, it becoming a job-seeker's market compared to the typical employer's market. This has led to 'The Great Resignation,' where ample opportunities for higher paying jobs have resulted in many employees resigning from their existing companies, some after long, illustrious careers. Open doors seem to be everywhere, beckoning you with LinkedIn messages, emails, and calls. In this market, I have decided to stay put with my current company, declining offers and patiently waiting through a season of uncertainty where I am not even sure if there will be a job for me on the other side. Why? It may sound foolish, but it's because this time around, I have decided to stay put until God tells me to move. When I decided to move with my family, setting aside potential opportunities that I had been dreaming of, all I had was a word from God saying, 'go, I will take care of it.' It's easy in the moment to take that leap of faith and get out of the boat like Peter, looking to Jesus and trusting Him. But almost eight months later, I sank below the water many times as my faith wavered and I started to sink, the temptation to take matters into my own hands a daily struggle, no different than an addict who fights their addiction every day. I knew God was good, that what He was working out was his best for me, and that his timing had a purpose, for my good and the good of all his people. I knew this, yet it is hard always to have unwavering faith in his timing and provision. It's much easier to think that He is not behind the scenes and that likely his answer is something I see in front of me.

I was likewise tempted the last time we went through a restructuring effort. Without praying or seeking guidance, I decided to make some moves and asked Him to bless my plans instead. If any of that had gone according to my plans, we would not have been in a place where we could accept this amazing adventure. At the time, I was flabbergasted and confused, but looking back now, I can see more clearly how the tapestry was woven. Similarly, this transition period of a few months has enabled me to rest through a pregnancy fraught with a series of my daughter's daycare viral infections and allowed me the time to finish this book which I know will be put aside again when the next baby arrives. If not for these few months, with a lot of help at home, I could not fathom having the time or energy to write with a toddler at home while pregnant and working an intense full-time job.

Again, His timing has turned out to be better than mine. Ephesians 6 describes the armor of God and specifically asks us to put on the shield of faith, which protects us against rulers, against the authorities, against the powers of this dark world, and against the spiritual forces of evil in the heavenly realms. Now that sounds a bit apocalyptic and dramatic for the workplace, but as I noted earlier, we spend a significant amount of our lives at work, not to mention the fact that very often, our sense of joy and fulfillment at work, or the lack thereof, often spills into all the other areas of our lives, not least our marriages and families. The worst is when work itself spills into these sacred times that should be spent with God, our families and loved ones, friends, or even ourselves and our hobbies. It is safe to assume then that it is very much in the devil's interest to keep you wholly distracted with the pursuit of money or success at the expense of all else. And so, we must guard ourselves with our faith and trust in God. I hope, my daughter, that you do a better job than I did (or will do). Remember that no recruiter, hiring manager, or a company offering a boatload of money will care about your long-term interests as much as our Good Father. Remember who He is;

"And he passed in front of Moses, proclaiming, "The Lord, the Lord, the compassionate and gracious God, slow to anger, abounding in love and faithfulness, maintaining love to thousands, and forgiving wickedness, rebellion, and sin..." - Exodus 34:6-7

This is how God described Himself (including his name) when given the chance. Not by any of his achievements but by his character, first and foremost being compassionate and gracious. I love that because it reminds me that God is goodness, love, and all that is kind and giving. How I should be able to trust that He will not want anything but a good life for me, the kind of life I will not regret on my deathbed. How I should be able to have faith in His plans and purpose.

I've come to realize that Faith is like any other muscle in the body. It needs exercise and attention, or else it withers away with time. We need to build ourselves up in the faith. And it's not one-and-done. We need to keep feeding it. Like going to the gym to ensure we stay fit, we must work to ensure our faith muscle is in top shape. If I said I wanted to run a Triathlon, let's say the workout equivalent of moving a mountain, is it enough for me to go to the gym one time? Of course not! But often, I treat my faith the way I used to treat new year's resolutions, contributing to gym revenues in January with nothing after that. No, daughter, we must keep working at it, pumping those weights, taking those daily walks, feeding mind, body, and soul with what God says about the situation, the person, or me. But when we start to sink, that's okay. Jesus pulls us out immediately. He will make sure we are not drowning first, and then He will calm the sea. His interest is in us.

12. a life of purpose

The Wife of Noble Character

"A wife of noble character who can find?
She is worth far more than rubies.
Her husband has full confidence in her
and lacks nothing of value.
She brings him good, not harm,
all the days of her life.
She selects wool and flax
and works with eager hands.
She is like the merchant ships,
bringing her food from afar.
She gets up while it is still night;
she provides food for her family
and portions for her female servants.
She considers a field and buys it;
out of her earnings she plants a vineyard.
She sets about her work vigorously;
her arms are strong for her tasks.
She sees that her trading is profitable,
and her lamp does not go out at night.
In her hand she holds the distaff
and grasps the spindle with her fingers.
She opens her arms to the poor
and extends her hands to the needy.
When it snows, she has no fear for her household;
for all of them are clothed in scarlet.
She makes coverings for her bed;
she is clothed in fine linen and purple.
Her husband is respected at the city gate,
where he takes his seat among the elders of the land.

She makes linen garments and sells them,
and supplies the merchants with sashes.
She is clothed with strength and dignity;
she can laugh at the days to come.
She speaks with wisdom,
and faithful instruction is on her tongue.
She watches over the affairs of her household
and does not eat the bread of idleness.
Her children arise and call her blessed;
her husband also, and he praises her:
"Many women do noble things,
but you surpass them all."
Charm is deceptive, and beauty is fleeting;
but a woman who fears the Lord is to be praised.
Honor her for all that her hands have done,
and let her works bring her praise at the city gate".
-Proverbs 31:10-31

When I first came across the famous 'Proverbs 31 woman', my first reaction was righteous indignation; indignation that in my thirty-something years on earth, including decades of attending church, not to mention the rigorous religious education I received in an all-girls Christian School, I had not once heard about this woman described in the Bible. Here was the answer to every tension and conflict between priorities, every question about self and identity, and every pursuit of purpose amidst conflicting desires. I have only myself to blame, of course. The answer I sought was always there- I just had to pick it up and read it.

Daughter, in *Breaking all the rules*, I went to great pains to tell you that you should not be discouraged by your circumstances, situations, or even characteristics. I would now like to remind you that you should be *greatly encouraged* by the very same things, as they equip you, uniquely, to make a great contribution to this world, to fulfill your God-given assignments in this lifetime, whether it is at home raising the next generation, or at work through leadership and accountability. Heaven is, and will be, the most diverse place we will ever encounter, filled with people who look different, from all sorts of backgrounds, united for one purpose. Every time we pray the Lord's prayer, we say, "(God) Your Will be done, on earth *as it is in heaven,"* which I find so encouraging; there is no reason that our schools, governments, workplaces, communities, and boardrooms can't be as diverse, bringing together unique perspectives and backgrounds for the common good of all.

As we speak, the world is going through a period of rapid change in lifestyle and energy; the type of change last seen during the technological revolution a few decades ago, or perhaps even as far back as the industrial revolution in the mid-19th century. One thing is clear. The world will look like a very different place in a matter of decades. Most companies in the world, whether at the forefront of energy supply or the far end as an energy consumer, are trying to work out for themselves exactly where they fit into this new world order. But one thing is clear. *No one can do it all.* If companies with tens, if not hundreds of billions of dollars in their arsenal routinely acknowledge that they cannot and should not 'do it all', choosing instead to play to their strengths, I am flabbergasted as to why we still, to this day, parrot the idea that we, mere humans, particularly women, with 24 hours of the day, expect ourselves to *do it all.*

Daughter, the rest of this letter is about my journey as someone who has chosen both to have a career and a family or dependents. As I have alluded to in my other letters, I wholeheartedly believe in the higher calling of full-time motherhood or housewife. But that was not my path. While I encourage you to find your purpose, I can only share my experiences related to my calling with you.

Proverbs 31 is introduced as being sayings of King Lemuel, a wise and powerful king who remembers the wise utterances and teachings of his mother. As such, the woman is not an actual woman, nor do I believe the tasks and responsibilities she assumes in her day-to-day life are a blueprint for all we should look to add to our plates. Rather she is a challenge to all women in that she embodies the characteristics of a Godly woman that certainly we can all look to aspire to, no matter what our chosen paths in life. She is not just a challenge or a series of possibilities; she is also *who we are already*, should we have the courage to embrace *who we were created to be.*

After her long list of accolades, she is noted to be, above all, a woman who fears the Lord, who no doubt lives according to his will, walking with

God through life, seeking his purpose and his guidance. All she does, at home, in the community, and in the workplace is driven and motivated by this reverence for God. She is a woman of honor, strength, and dignity; a virtuous woman. If married, she is a blessing to her husband. She is hard-working and industrious, clearly with a good head for business, diligent, resourceful, and organized, planning for future needs. She is not just concerned with her household but extends her generosity to the community, generous in her giving to the needy. She is wise and possesses knowledge and instruction. If she is a mother, she is a blessing to her children.

When I read this passage, three women come to my mind; my mother, my mother-in-law and my grandmother. One had a series of jobs, one had a career and became a business owner, and one was a full-time stay-at-home wife and mother. That is how I know beyond a doubt that this passage is less about the list of responsibilities held by this woman, and more about her character, something that is of much more interest to God. I know that if I could embody and emulate even a part of the life led by these three women, my children will call me blessed. Contrary to the glorification of 'doing it all' or celebrating 'superwomen' who have it all, I take great inspiration from this passage which gently shows me all that I am and could be as a woman for God, all the possibilities, but also comforting me that no matter what our calling is in life, as long as we are walking with God, according to his unique calling on our lives, I am already that woman.

Be Intentionally Purposeful

I have spent my fair share of time complaining about the fact that I felt that I was carrying a disproportionate share of the mental load in the house, as it is referred to these days. This is anything from organizing the needs of the house (think of buying milk and diapers before they run out in the middle of the night), ordering gas to be delivered, pest control, managing contracts and household projects, finding a daycare for our daughter, making sure she has clothes and shoes that fit her at all times, finding a pediatrician, making appointments for well-checks and vaccinations to name just a few that come to mind (wow that popped out pretty easily!). But in recent months or even years, I have come to revise and soften my stance on this. Of course, a biblical but hard-to-swallow answer would be that we are to be a helper to our husbands, but my rationale was slightly different, perhaps less biblical and more logical.

At my company, except for some very specialized technical roles, most jobs can be quite general in scope; finance, commercial, human resources, etc., and I suspect the same is true for most industries. Of course, there are varying degrees of expertise for these roles, but most people can do most jobs with a bit of training, coaching, and understanding if the underlying gifting is there. It's hardly rocket science (except, as I said, for those roles, which are varying degrees of rocket science). That being said, not everyone will do every job to the same level of excellence or standards for one very simple reason; we all have our strengths and perform best when we play to them. Some of us are naturally quantitative thinkers, where numbers are our friend. Still, others can read a room and build a rapport with someone, building a friendship while delivering a very difficult message. Some love details and others love to operate at thirty thousand feet, seeing patterns and interconnections. The list goes on. It follows logically, therefore, that the company, or even society as a whole, benefits most when we do what we are most gifted at, playing to our strengths and gifts and talents. Gender roles aside, I feel that idea translates to the home, where we must contribute to the household in areas where we are strongest. That would be the most efficient outcome.

What a simple thought with profound implications regarding how we approach all that we do, whether at work or home. Plus, I often use this thought to excuse why I only step into the kitchen to boil an egg or make myself coffee; why would I make society that much more inefficient in time and talent management by trying to cook?

Purpose, specifically *my purpose as it relates to work or career,* is something I have often thought about, invading my thoughts in the quiet of the night. It's probably a question I will continue asking all through my life, perhaps only receiving the final answer on the other side. But until then, a culmination of prayer, reflection, reading the Bible, and inspiration has given me at least a partial answer that I feel is a sufficient guidepost to keep me on the right track.

The first and most obvious is, of course, the creation mandate; the solid set of instructions given to men *and* women after creation as to what their operational mandate on earth is;

> *"Then God said, "Let us make mankind in our image, in our likeness, so that they may rule over the fish in the sea and the birds in the sky, over the livestock and all the wild animals, and over all the creatures that move along the ground." So God created mankind in his own image, in the image of God he created them; male and female he created them. God blessed them and said to them, "Be fruitful and increase in number; fill the earth and subdue it. Rule over the fish in the sea and the birds in the sky and over every living creature that moves on the ground." - Genesis 1: 26-28*

When we hear terms like 'ruling' and 'subduing,' the natural inclination is to think of a king lording over his kingdom. But as any leader worth a dime would tell you, with the heavy burden of leadership comes a responsibility for the wellbeing of your subjects, or else your kingdom will surely not be long-lasting. Or as Uncle Ben told Spiderman, 'with great power comes great responsibility.

I find this bible passage so significant. I am no scholar, and my interpretation is one of a simple woman reading the Bible, but I think it is really meaningful that the mandate in verse 28 above was given to both men *and* women. As soon as the next chapter, we see God giving specific instructions to Adam (man) alone, and the mandate could so easily have been included here, but I take heart that it was especially included here and given as an instruction to the duo. Of course, it does not get into roles and responsibilities; as we know, men and women have very different roles to play in the biological process of 'multiplying,' but the general mandate is clear.

We were not put on earth to be idle, and the mandate is two-fold in scope; humanity (or relationships) and resources. From the perspective of community, we have a responsibility firstly, whether at home, raising children, taking care of our family and dependents or outside the home, in the church, in our towns, or whatever community you may influence. We also have a responsibility from the perspective of managing the vast resources that we have dominion over. All women have a great contribution they can make in their lifetime according to their unique calling. The Proverbs 31 woman illustrates just a few of these ways. In fact, I don't believe there are small callings in life, whether you are a housewife managing the thermostat or water taps in your home responsibly or you are solving the world's problems through science and technology, you could be leaving a legacy and footprint that can last for generations.

One only needs to look around the world today to realize that there is much work to be done. Yet, within such a broad mandate and a wide slate of responsibility for such a scope of work, it is easy to get lost in a quest for meaning and purpose in everyday tasks. Where is a life of purpose or meaning when neck deep in a budget report, a sales pitch to a client, or processing an invoice, among other everyday tasks? If we aren't rescuing whales or saving a life in an operating theatre, are we falling short of our mandate and calling?

I believe not. Thankfully, Jesus illustrated this with a story that cuts right to the heart of how we are to occupy the days of our life and our calling as Christians.

In the story, we hear of a wealthy master who embarks on a long journey. Before he leaves, he calls to him three of his servants and entrusts them with a unique responsibility, presumably in proportion to their abilities. To one servant, he entrusts five talents (or gold or silver coins), to the second servant, he gives two talents, and to the third servant, he gives one talent. During their master's absence, the first two servants, who were given five and two talents respectively, were good stewards of what they were given, invested wisely, and doubled what was given to them. The third servant unwisely went away, dug a hole, and buried the talent given to him, yielding no returns. When the master returned, he was well pleased with the first two servants. "Well done, good and faithful servant," the master said to each of them. "You were faithful with a few things; I will put you in charge of many things. Enter into the joy of your master" (Matthew 25:21). The servant who was fearful and negligent, however, was swiftly reprimanded by his master, who called him "wicked, lazy, and worthless." His talent was taken and given to the one with ten talents, and he himself was thrown out of his master's presence (Matthew 25:30).

The story is simple yet clear. We are the servants, and we are each given our unique gifts, abilities, and resources to steward in this lifetime. Some are given much, others little. Though not all have the same, the responsibility for good stewardship of what *has* been placed into our hands is clear. With that narrowing of focus, it becomes much easier to look around at what we have been entrusted with, the opportunities around us, and where we *have* been placed to find our calling in the narrow bridge that brings perfect harmony between our talents and our circumstances. In other words, I have found that as long as I am in a close relationship with God, seeking his wisdom and will before taking that next immediate step (which may feel like a small or even insignificant step), my purpose is found in being a good steward of the here and now. This has freed me from the obsessive need to find greater purpose and meaning in every department or company that I work for and realize that purpose, meaning and fulfillment in life are found in faithfully carrying out whatever assignment God has entrusted me with *for that day*. The key to fulfillment in the work of your hands then becomes a close relationship with the God who has given that unique calling in life and who, at the right time, will guide you to greater levels of responsibility.

We have all heard the cliche, 'when you love what you do, you never work a day in your life'. I love what I do, but work is still work. It can be fulfilling, but it is no less demanding, challenging, or tiring, and I certainly can't equate it to sitting at a beach reading a book and sipping a mojito. But one thing I have observed is that is when the magic happens, there is a perfectly harmonious relationship between your unique strengths and gifts and the work you are engaged in. It doesn't feel like you are trying to fit a square peg into a round hole. Daughter, if you do not experience that strange mix of peace and excitement at what you do, I encourage you to keep praying and asking for wisdom and direction so that the right door might become clear to you or ask for wisdom and insights to see your current circumstances in a new way. Stay patient, planted, and bloom where you are until God opens that door for you. God intends for us to live full lives, maximizing our gifts. There is no sense of satisfaction quite like looking at what you produce, whether an architectural miracle or an excel spreadsheet. I have left work late more often than I can count, but on those days where it is because I was working hard at something that I was really enjoying, I am still buzzing with a strange high when I get home, almost unable to sleep despite extreme exhaustion, my brain filled with anticipation and plans for the next morning when I will pick up that piece of work again. I still recall with fondness the Saturday I spent with one of my best friends many years ago, trying to value a chicken farm business she founded, debating "how do we depreciate the chicken?" Even as I pen down this thought, I realize how much of a dork that makes me sound like.

The financial implications of working and having that steady income stream have also allowed me to crystallize my calling in life. One of the things I most love about my career is that it allows me the capacity to not just take care of my parents and family but also meet financial needs when I see them. Of course, that is not to say that I could not do so with my husband's income; after all, we manage the budget as a household, but perhaps it is whatever that was instilled in me in those young days, seeing my father give to every needy person at every traffic light, that makes me want to say yes to pretty much any genuine request that comes my way, to the extent that I am able and feeling a sense of joy and satisfaction that I am doing so with the fruit of my labor. Some people love giving their time and energy to ministry. I love using my hard-earned income to give to ministry work, knowing that even though I am sweating it out in a fluorescent-lit cubicle, someone is using those funds to go on a mission trip to build a house or church in a faraway land. I hope that one day, society will catch up to and stay-at-home mothers will be paid their fair share of wages for childcare responsibilities in a way that will allow them to more directly enjoy the financial benefits of their hard work in addition to the joy they receive through their service to their families.

One of the most direct instructions Jesus gave us in the New Testament follow shortly after the parable of the talents, where he says to feed the hungry, give water to the thirsty, show hospitality to strangers and aliens, and provide clothing and ministry to the needy. Elsewhere in the New Testament, we are told to look after the widows and the orphans. If we can't even look after our needs or the needs of our families, how can we look after others? The financial blessings and prosperity that God provides is yet another resource given to us to steward well, to be re-directed to the appropriate place to take care of his people. At the end of my life, I want to be able to say that I lived my life as a river, not a reservoir. Water flows freely through and down the river, nourishing everything along its path. On the other hand, the reservoir captures and withholds all water coming to it upstream, leaving dry lands downstream. I think river living is the only way to live as though you are the first two servants, the good stewards.

"What good is it for someone to gain the whole world, yet forfeit their soul?" -Mark 8:36

In my earlier letter, I cautioned against tying our identity to anything other than Christ, with work being one of the most tempting mistresses. There is a quote by an unknown author which says, *"You may get to the very top of the ladder and then find it has not been leaning against the right wall,"* which reminds me of the same thought again.

King Solomon is often credited as being one of, if not the wisest man who ever lived. It is written that when God personally appeared to him in a dream and asked him what he wanted, instead of riches or the defeat of his enemies, he asked for wisdom to rule God's people well. Well pleased by this selfless request, God is said to have personally granted him his wish. Under his rule, the united nation of Israel prospered, going on to attain its highest level of wealth and prosperity in its history. Less inspiring was the fact that he had about a thousand wives and concubines, which frankly doesn't seem very wise to me, but that's just my opinion. Perhaps he was considered the wisest of them all by his *male* counterparts. Solomon wrote one of my favorite books in the Bible, the book of Proverbs, which offers a multitude of wisdom and insights for a good life, so much so that sometimes I come across a quotable quote in a gift shop or book and when I look up the source, I find that it originates from the book of Proverbs. However, he also wrote one of my least favorite books of the Bible, the book of Ecclesiastes, which I find to be a depressing, albeit enlightening, read. In the latter, Solomon, after a lifetime of attaining the highest levels of wisdom, wealth, and sovereignty (where he was not bound by the laws of the land and could do as he pleased), having pursued and experienced every pleasure afforded to man, be it wine or women, finally concluded that *it can, if we are not careful, be meaningless.* The word 'meaningless' is used 38 times, taken from the Hebrew word 'hevel,' which means smoke or vapor. That is not to say that our lives have no value, but a reminder that our lives and all we do on earth are fleeting, like smoke or vapor, and in that context, do not last. No matter how much was attained, none of these could satisfy or provide fulfillment. These things only have value in the context of a relationship with God, who is the only source of fulfillment.

Does this mean wealth and possessions are bad, leading to an unfulfilled life? Thankfully, he goes on to note that "Moreover, when God gives someone wealth and possessions, and the ability to enjoy them, to accept their lot and be happy in their toil—this is a gift of God" (Ecclesiastes 5:19). I love this verse because it is both a reminder that ultimately God is the source of happiness and joy, but also because happiness and contentment are described as being a *gift* from God, not something to manifest through our own will and effort, but something we can ask God to gift to us. I think the key to finding fulfillment in all that you do then is to stop slaving away for that next promotion, that next rung in the ladder, hoping that maybe when you get to the top, you may finally rest easy and instead look to God for that fulfillment and contentment, the ultimate source. He may take you to the C-Suite because it uniquely positions you to help people He places along your path, or through your giving, or to make an impact in your organization in some unique way. Or He may cut back your responsibilities so that you have more time to spend using your gifts serving others in church ministry or finally have more time for your spouse, parents, grandparents, or children. Or perhaps He closes a door to take you out of a stressful career path which ultimately will affect your health and cut short your ability to fulfill your purpose down the line. Either way, He can give us the ability to be content and fulfilled with the path that He has set apart for us, that reflects His best for us.

So Daughter, be ambitious! Dream! Aspire! But let God use your ambition for his purpose, and He will direct you to the best possible life that He intends for you and give you the ability to enjoy the fruit of your hard work.

Rest in the Lord

"Come to me, all you who are weary and burdened, and I will give you rest. Take my yoke upon you and learn from me, for I am gentle and humble in heart, and you will find rest for your souls. For my yoke is easy, and my burden is light." - Matthew 11:28-30

Daughter, our time together is at an end for now. We have been on quite a journey together. I hope that by now you are, at least, somewhat encouraged.

I end this last letter celebrating all that you are and all that you do. I see you work diligently with all your tasks. I know that you seek to serve your family, loved ones, colleagues, and leaders, even when there is no reward for your hard work. I see the heart you have for your spouse, your children, your parents, siblings, colleagues, and your community.

But let us not take on more than we were meant to carry. The heaviest of these is thinking that we can control the outcomes of the universe through our actions, whether at home or work. Doing so will only keep us in a prison of stress, anxiety, and complete exhaustion. Jesus reminds us gently that "[we] are worried and upset about many things, but few things are needed—or indeed only one," and that is to sit at his feet, resting, listening, and enjoying his presence. All other things will work themselves out in time. So let us work hard as we are instructed to do, diligent in the tasks and responsibilities given to us. After all, it is nothing short of our mandate on earth, remembering our instructions in Colossians 3:23-24; "Whatever you do, work at it with all your heart, as working for the Lord, not for human masters, since you know that you will receive an inheritance from the Lord as a reward. It is the Lord Christ you are serving". Let us use our gifts and talents responsibly as good stewards in whatever area of responsibility we have been entrusted with, not to win the praise and acceptance of others, but to please our generous Father who cares for us.

But above all, my darling daughter, rest in the Lord. In this season of waiting, I have come to learn the hard way that every time I wrestle for control, to take the lead, I take on the burden of trying to control the uncontrollable. All I end up achieving is stress, anxiety, and frustration. I cannot control human hearts; I cannot even control the safety of my loved ones. I cannot control the choices my children will make one day, and as I have found, I cannot control the opportunities available to me in the workplace. All I can do is pray that I wake up every day grateful for another day of life, ask God to give me the wisdom to do my best, and thank Him for filling my cup again. Jesus offers us a better way, asking us to rely on His strength, His sovereignty over all things, instead of our limited strength.

Most of all, when I rest in Him instead of on my abilities and strength, I can put down burdens I am not meant to carry and enjoy the peace and contentment He always desired for us. And what is that, you may ask?

I believe it is a life of walking through a garden full of resources, where there is no lack, no competition for supplies and opportunities, a daily relationship with a living God, a peaceful relationship with your partner in marriage, perhaps children and grandchildren, community and family, and good stewardship of all the responsibility we have been entrusted with as we enjoy the fruit of our labor, with contentment and joy, in a world where nothing is impossible.

Daughter, that sounds like a life that I want to live.

Nihara Guruge

Nihara Guruge is available for interviews. For more information contact:

info@advbooks.com

To purchase additional copies of these books, visit our bookstore at:
www.advbookstore.com

Orlando, Florida, USA
"we bring dreams to life"™
www.advbookstore.com

Made in the USA
Columbia, SC
15 April 2023

15122843R00089